REFLECTIONS OF *Success*

Principles of Christian Administration

A Tribute to Janet Trout

REFLECTIONS OF SUCCESS

by Janet Trout

ISBN 0-912315-81-4

All Scripture quotations in this book are from the King James Version of the Bible unless otherwise identified.

Printed in United States of America.

Order from:

Kent Christian Center
1761 N. DuPont Hwy.
Dover, DE 19901

Table of Contents

Editor's Note

During the late 1970's and early 1980's Christian day schools have become a very integral part of the ministry of the Church. There are an estimated twelve to fifteen schools beginning each week. With this rise of Christian schools emerges a need for the publication of material which addresses the administrative aspect of Christian Education from a scriptural perspective.

Leadership is a calling from God. Leaders are not born, they are made. Leadership is not for everyone, many do not want the pressures and the loneliness which so distinctly marks this position—leadership. Those in administrative positions want to be strong leaders, so that they will be able to communicate effectively with those who are following.

There are certain principles, when applied, that will help make you the leader God intends for you to be. The Alumni Association of Kent Christian College has compiled various writings and transcribed messages given by Janet Trout, who has served as the Director of Kent Christian College and Academy since 1975. The success of her ministry is built upon many years of experience and also the many hours which she has personally invested in reading and studying principles of management from the business world and joining these with the Word of God.

Sister Trout's comments in response to the publication of this book were, "I don't know if I am successful or not, I am still working on it!" The many phone calls and letters received on a daily basis speak for themselves. We, the editorial staff of this publication, are also Kent Christian Center staff members, and we can attest that her life exemplifies her words. The principles of this book are not mere words to her, but are policies and precedents she lives by as she works side-by-side with Brother Trout leading people in two churches, a Christian Academy and College.

We hope that the time and money invested in this publication will encourage and help other administrators as they strive to be effective leaders in the Kingdom of God.

Diana Walters

Foreword

Leadership can be a very lonely position. Any leader in spiritual things must be a follower of the Spirit. The leader is the physical embodiment of God's presence. Paul, the Apostle, said, "Follow me as I follow Christ." The follower must have an object that is tangible to follow. The leader must be able to see Him who is invisible. He who has never learned to follow is a very dangerous leader for he has rejected the very foundation upon which true leadership is established. The true key to leadership is not one's might or power—but meekness. (Meekness is not weakness but power in control.)

Real leadership does not make his fellow man feel inferior, uncomfortable, intimidated, but rather secure and comfortable. Real leadership will come to the front when the need calls for him yet the real leader is willing to decline to the position of a follower when one more capable evolves. Success in leadership is often doing that which another has refused to do.

The secret is to make each man feel he is important to the success of the program, especially if his job is a surface job or out of sight. Remember, the proper function of the internal organs is as important to the well-being of the body as the external organs.

Many want to be leaders but are not ready to assume the responsibilities of leadership. This is true on the job, in the home, in school, and in church. God deliver us from title and office seekers and give us productive leaders whether they be male or female.

In the following pages Janet will share with you many of the tried and proven qualities of a true leader. She has shared these ideas with thousands in special seminars and public meetings, and now with you—the reader.

Janet is a woman among women—few women know how to fill the role of an effective leader in management, administration, counseling in the office and then get into her automobile and on her way home be transformed into a loving wife and mother by the time she hits the doorstep. All these traits and attributes are bundled up into a beautiful 118 pound package I call my wife.

Wayne R. Trout

Introduction

Since I was a child, I have been awed by the power of leadership. Early in my teens I felt, as all young people do, the tug of influence brought to bear by "peer pressure." As my life and ministry developed it became apparent that any successes I enjoyed could be attributed to those whose models I followed and not to any original good on my part.

This was, to me, a revelation. If so many good people had taught me so much by silent example, how much more could I learn if I applied myself to wisdom? Then, there are the corporate giants that continually intrigued me. The revelation began to expand. If the principles of success worked well for businesses, why would they not work well for the most important business on earth? People, generally speaking, are the same whether on a Christian school staff or in a corporate office—that is with the exception of those who have been mellowed by the indwelling of the Holy Ghost.

I soon found out by experience that most people want to be trained, instructed and told where their boundaries are—which brought me to yet another conclusion. Most problems I found myself frustrated by were a result of my failure to communicate valuable information such as: what are my expectations, are there deadlines, and how far can a worker go?

I noticed when I started "speaking up" and making

myself clear, delegating and transmitting, wonderful things began to happen. Workers who were secure, talented people did not feel threatened, I was not frustrated—still tired, but not frustrated!

The final phase of my revelation dawned on me when I was awakened to the "ministry of transmission." As the value of administrative leadership became apparent by staff interfaces from day to day, I determined to transmit it to the college students.

God said to Moses, "What is that in thine hand?" He experienced the awesome responsibility of leadership.

Finally, it is not the worker over yonder, across the country that will do you good. Take what you have. They will be loyal. Try not to import help. Use those who "come in" under you—train them! You can do it, you have it in your hand! But beware, to make it work, you have to be willing to work at it! You have lived below your potential long enough!

The faint-hearted, people pleasers should stop here, but if you are eager to break out of a rut and organize. . .read on!

Happy Leading!

Janet Trout

The Administrator

Chapter 1

Administration

WORDS OF WISDOM for those involved in church staff management.

In the following pages you will find a variety of subjects represented. The Sunday school staff is faced with the challenge of integrating its activities with the other departments of the church. In order to do so successfully, the basic rules of staff interfaces must be addressed.

Since management is needed in all departments, by all leaders, I shall refer to that position of leadership as a "manager." It could represent the Director of Christian Education managing those serving under him. The Sunday school superintendent is a manager, as is every departmental superintendent, etc.

Recognizing one's place within the chain of command and functioning according to the rules is bound to give every worker a measure of success, peace, and confidence in his ability to do God's great work.

The following text is not elaborated on in full detail, however, enough information is given to expose the necessity of observing the rules faithfully.

PRACTICAL MANAGEMENT – Church Staff Interfaces

The Grapevine

The church grapevine should not be used to pass along information to workers. REASON: There is a loss of accuracy in the rumor mill; other information is added, and the bias of those spreading the rumor color the communication and either weaken its message or add impetus in the wrong places.

As a manager, you can use the grapevine to keep informed about workers' concerns and potential problems that may be developing.

Meetings

Schedule meetings late in the day when a built-in time limit would be useful. This is good for "light" planning and coordination; however, more serious sessions should be held in the morning when minds and spirits are fresh.

Reorganization

New administrators: BEWARE!! Don't begin large-scale reorganizations immediately.

> **PROBLEM:** You may take action for the wrong reasons (to show that someone decisive is in charge or to give yourself a few months' grace before your superiors demand results).
>
> **BETTER WAY:** Do not make structural changes without the counsel and approval of the pastor and the faithful workers who put the brick and mortar together before you arrived. Wait until the strengths and weaknesses of all key workers are known by you.

Clean & organized

Signs That A Manager Is Not Delegating Enough:

a. The mechanics of the organization become tangled when the manager is away, and progress slows down.
b. Friction, low morale, and lack of initiative characterize the staff.
c. Workers defer all decisions on problems to the manager.
d. New ideas do not come from workers.
e. The manager is irritable and complains when a subordinate and/or group's work is not up to expectations.
f. A manager sees a worker's potential based on salary vs. volunteer.
g. A manager is perpetually frustrated by unfinished tasks.

The Self-Proclaimed Indispensable Manager/Worker

How to spot workers/managers who try to make themselves irreplaceable:

a. Their offices and rooms are a mess. Every nook and cranny is chock full of papers, samples, material and information needed by their department. They are the only ones who can find anything.
b. They carry briefcases more than six inches wide. These managers load up with homework because running the operation "single handedly" demands every waking hour! Tsk! Tsk!!
c. Their days are filled with co-workers questions. Co-workers don't take initiative because the manager has withheld vital information.

How to stop this behavior:

a. Train workers to operate within a basic format that is

consistent throughout every department. Someone else should be able to walk in, find everything and take over in case of illness, death, or walk-out.

b. Demand that all messes, including the disarray in the manager's office, be cleaned up within a specified time period.

c. Reorganize their department, delegating authority to responsible workers. Work must never stop or be slowed by the absence of a single person. One-person control of a department is a dangerous bottle neck that can choke the flow of vital information and breed discontent in the other workers, especially subordinates who are expected to perform a task even when deprived of critical insights.

How To Know What's Really Going On!

The trouble with much of the information Christian administrators get is that it is second hand. It is filtered first through various levels of biased reporting.

To get a first hand feel of how things are *really* going, spend an unannounced day with a staff member, going along on the normal rounds. Listen and ask questions of everyone you meet. Prearranged visits have their place but they have their problems. They are *not* an effective way to get the true picture. If your visit is preannounced, the desk and closet will be stuffed with unfinished work and problems will be swept under the rug instead of dealt with.

Alternative: use less conspicuous people as surrogate eyes and ears. (Example: a fellow staff member on the same level you are investigating; one you can trust to be honest, objective, and knowledgeable on the subject under observation. Debrief them upon their return for their impression and observations.)

Listening For Bad News

A common roadblock to good communications is a staff member who does not want to be the one to tell the supervisor or administrator the bad news. No one does! A good administrator will make it easy for staff members to discuss problems without "emotional reporting" (which is usually a result of one feeling his position and/or authority is being threatened or under fire). Encourage staff members to mention dubious situations to you. One of the following will happen:

a. You will have the opportunity to lay invalid fears to rest, stop a rumor, and set the record straight.
b. You will get hold of vital information while a problem is small, localize it and deal with it before it becomes widespread. Remember: you are not God and you do not know all things. Discernment is not to be misappropriated in these types of situations. A good administrator will look for the staff to keep him/her well informed.

Positive approach: receive the bad news calmly. Don't jump to conclusions—listen for personal biases as they surface in the report. Weed out ulterior motives in the reporter (That's a different problem!). Get to the heart of the matter.

Never jump on the person who reports a serious problem. If a rebuke is needed, never do it in a meeting or when anyone else is present. Hold off even if the reporter is responsible for the problem. Get all of the facts.

Dealing with older staff members vs. young, aggressive ones: older people tend to be a bit thin-skinned in meetings.

Aggressive young staff members may grate sensitive egos, but they keep an organization vital. An administrator that faces up to tough questions is more likely to maintain the respect of most staff member.

Planning Sessions

It is best to hold a few good ones than many inconsequential ones! Biannually review the group's strengths and weaknesses. For optimum results: take two or three key people out to lunch or dinner and listen to them. Review and revise plans. A wise man will change his mind, a fool never does.

Ask well-worded questions and listen carefully to each response. Weigh very carefully the origin of the answer: is it based on carnal or spiritual interpretation of a situation?

Traps That Prevent Problem Solving

Those who do not succeed in solving problems fail because:

a. They cannot tolerate the ambiguity associated with a complex problem; they believe all problems must be clear cut. Problems within a church family and/or staff members are not always that simplistic. There are no pat answers. Most problems in a church-school-staff situation have several tributaries, some carnal, some very natural, some spiritual and extremely complex. Dealing with them will require prayer, wisdom, sensitivity to personal feelings and a double dose of the discerning of spirits.

b. They stick to a preconceived belief and reinterpret inconsistent data to fit it.

c. They hesitate to ask questions for fear of appearing ignorant.
d. They give into unrealistic anxiety about failing.
e. They overemphasize aspects of the problem related to their position and department.
f. They tend to be too logical; they focus on a solution too quickly rather than spend time analyzing the problem.
g. They fail to be innovative and will not break rules of tradition; they rely on tested solutions, failing to realize what scriptural responses may be appropriate (apology, forgiveness, longsuffering, kindness, etc.), which may be "out of character" for them.
h. They rely on "own understanding" ("Lean not to thine understanding". . .) and ignore common sense. They fail to seek counsel for an outside point of view.

Myths About Dealing With Workers

a. *MYTH #1:* Never do anything that will cause someone to dislike you.
REALITY: Your job is to please God, your immediate superior, make proper judgments, be honest, fair, and merciful, *not* please everyone or impress them. Certain goals will be reached only at the expense of your personal goals.
b. *MYTH #2:* Managers, supervisors and/or administrators must seek approval from entire staff before making a decision. Don't ruffle anyone's feathers!
REALITY: Good church administration often requires making undemocratic decisions. They are easier to make when you keep a safe distance from the staff.
c. *MYTH #3:* Staff members should understand the

reasons for a Christian administrator's actions.
REALITY: This is often impossible. To explain is to reveal personal intricacies of other's lifes; many times it is futile. Attempting to win acceptance makes the administrator seem indecisive or unsure.

d. *MYTH #4:* An open door policy where workers can discuss personal problems is effective.
REALITY: Knowledge of an employee's personal life will influence your feelings about the person's work. Stay out of workers' personal lives unless you are invited via the medium of counsel, and be sure then, it is your appropriate role.
Equally wise: do not divulge your personal problems to subordinates. It leaves them with the feeling that you cannot manage your job. Your credibility suffers, therefore, your effectiveness is also impaired.

e. *MYTH #5:* Departmental heads, administrators and/or supervisors should be experts on everything in their department or they will lose credibility with those under them.
REALITY: Managers who try to keep their hands on every activity are perceived as interfering and robbing subordinates of their initiative.
A good manager is not necessarily one who knows everything; rather, is one who is wise enough to gather around him/herself workers who do—then give them liberty to perform in their various fields of expertise.

Characteristics of Truly Committed Workers

a. They get a great deal of personal satisfaction from their accomplishments.
b. They totally immerse themselves in a project (tip: a

brief break is needed to recover emotionally before a new assignment).

c. They assess the feasibility of a task and speak up when they think the odds are bad. Uncommitted workers take on anything without caring whether it is possible.
d. They back up and cover for co-workers and supervisors without concern for who is responsible or received the credit.
e. They understand the objectives and proceed to reach the goal without constant prodding and checking by their superior.
f. They feel apprehension and anxiety at the possibility of failure; unhesitatingly ask for help from supervisors and/or administrators.

Tidbits

a. Intelligent disagreement should be encouraged. Much of it will be constructive and useful for working flaws out of the system. A knowledgeable person is rarely entirely wrong.
b. Responsibility. . .but no authority! Even supervisors with only a few subordinates need to feel they have some measure of power, not just responsibility. Supervisors who function as mere intermediaries to transmit instructions from above will curtail productivity because there is no power to affect progress.
c. Unwillingness to discipline marginal workers can hurt a supervisor/administrator's effectiveness. REASON: Discipline confirms performance norms and standards of conduct. Failure to apply the standards shakes the other worker's sense of fairness in the system.
d. Combatting Criticism: When others criticize new ideas

too quickly, ask them to state two positive points for the idea before they can state the negative point. This is also helpful for a staff member who suffers from low self-esteem. Ask them to name at least two points about themselves before accepting the negative one. When a worker is "smarting" from the prospect of impending failure, ask them to recall at least two major projects in which they were successful.

Getting Others To Act—The Pros and Cons!

Every successful administrator knows how to influence others—his own boss (to get approval for projects and decisions), peers (to get support for programs), subordinates (to get the job done). Less understood are the powers and limitations of basic influence strategies:

a. *PRO:* Direct orders—get things done *fast,* just the way the administrator wants them done.
   CON: Direct orders breed ill will and subordinates comply only when the boss is around.
b. *PRO:* Negotiation requires giving something to get something else.
   CON: There is little flexibility because every change must be negotiated.
c. *PRO:* Enlisting support from others is done best on the basis of friendship or need.
   CON: The beneficiary now owes the other person a favor and the other person may renege on the committment.
d. *PRO:* Building on others' ideas involves others and commits them to the task.
   CON: Much time is spent resolving conflicts. Decision

making suffers because of the large number of people involved. The project may be derailed if others lose interest.

Preparing For The Future

There's room at the top! Identify promising administrative talent early, then nurture it for future purposes. In the next few years the supply of top management talent in church administration will fall short of the demand. It is far more advisable to raise up and train loyal, local talent than to import and employ people who do not share a pastor's vision, philosophy, and convictions. Be sure to get the pastor's approval before singling out an individual for this purpose. BEWARE: training and developing is a slow process, don't get discouraged.

Breaking Level Barriers: When and Why?

There are times when a top level administrator should break traditional rules and go down through the channels to subordinates two or three levels below.

A. Direct contact can be useful WHEN:

1. The administrator needs a clear view of what is going on at lower levels, unfiltered and undistorted by middle manager's perception and interests;
2. There is reason to doubt the middle managers are portraying top administrators accurately to those below them;
3. Lower level workers must be assessed for future promotions (or demotions). Top level admnistration must listen to middle managers, but not limit him/herself entirely to that evaluation;

4. Lower level workers merit special recognition.
a. *WARNING:* Direct contacts like these should be *rationed.*

B. *CONSEQUENCES* of side stepping (BREAKING) level barriers too often are:

1. The middle manager's status and authority can be undermined;
2. The top administrators are sucked into messy interpersonal and interdepartmental battles that ought to be resolved at lower levels. Getting involved in lower level problems can damage an administrator's reputation and compromise presumed impartiality. Top level administrators should mediate a conflict only after it has smouldered and when high level intervention seems to assure a quick solution.

Chapter 2

Effective Leadership

Being in the position of a leader does not make you a leader any more than walking into a barn makes you a horse. The appointment to a position of leadership is only the beginning. As soon as the appointment is announced you will begin to see different responses from various quarters. People who were close to you may become remote. Old friends may feel shut out because you are now on a "higher level" and they "didn't make it." You will encounter a broad range of responses from people you have worked around for many years—with no problem. Some of these attitudes may include hostility and suspicion. Do not be surprised to find an old friend hoping you make a mess! I know, "Brethren, these things ought not so to be," but, brethren, they do happen!

Those appointed to a position of leadership must earn the respect of those whom they lead by providing positive influence through the use of specific skills and methods.

FINDING THE KEY

The key to effective leadership is found in human need; the need to survive, to relate to those around us, to have individual identity, self-esteem and acceptance. To separate these human needs, simply because we function in relationship to spiritual matters, is a mistake.

It would be nice to know that God's people could totally abandon all personal pride and needs in order to do His work; however, it is an unrealistic dream. Even in God's work, consideration must be given to the ever-present human need. To run, roughshod, over it is the certain demise of effective leadership.

Conversely, to ignore the needs of leaders themselves is a tragic mistake. One who is called upon to lead must continually refurbish and replenish himself. An ongoing program of personal training and self-help must be maintained, as well as spiritual maintenance. The leader of God's people, at any level, asks for trouble when he becomes carnal, resorting to "weapons of warfare" that do not belong in His work.

It is never wise to become so goal-oriented that the people's needs are ignored. An effective leader must strike a balance between goals and people. One without the other is incomplete. To destroy the people while reaching a goal accomplishes nothing.

COLLABORATION!

Collaboration! Combining the finest from each mind on the team. Group genius! Instead of a "one man show," the leader turns his staff into an effective team, extracting the best from each. Individual staff members will be more oriented to the goals of the organization and its success if they are permitted to participate in making decisions about those goals and how they can be reached. It also vents the steam that seems to build pressure if the leader assumes a position of power and dictatorship.

Effective leadership tends to move down through an organization, and with it the team spirit. On the contrary, status-seeking leaders widen the gap between themselves and the workers. Results: alienation.

Leaders should not solve problems for people, but learn the skill of helping others find solutions for their problems. The counseling function of a leader provides a process whereby subordinates solve problems on their own in a relatively safe manner. By building a *problem solving team,* the job is finished, quicker than when a "one man show" limits the potential. Besides, if a leader has all the answers, he would have to be omniscient, having an inexhaustible source of knowledge and experience.

RETALIATION

Retaliate! That is the most common response to criticism and/or opposition. Leaders are, for the most part, people of strong will. It takes a lot of prayer and restraint to refrain from retaliation when opposition is felt. Pray! Tell God about your enemies. Report them to the "Throne." Furthermore, you are not as vulnerable on your knees as when you stand rigid and high, becoming a ready target. Many ground wars, fought man to man, hand to hand, were won by men who inched their way along on their stomachs and knees. Those who chose to stand up and/or run were mowed down by rapid fire from the enemies' M-16! Progress is not always measured by speed.

The worst thing a leader can do is reduce himself to grovel in the day-to-day conflict of people. If you spend all your energy and time fighting back, there will be no strength or time for the challenge at hand.

The President said, "If you can't take the heat, get out of the kitchen." A leader will feel the heat! He must learn how to properly respond to it.

OPPOSITION

There *will* be opposition. There *will* be criticism. The leader must face each occurrence on his knees, and with clear thinking. Do not loose your rationale by getting caught up in the conflict. You had better learn to think, pray, and run all at the same time.

President Johnson said, "If it ain't broke, don't fix it." Things that work well and produce good results do not need to be changed. There is no need to try to impress people by upsetting everything and everyone!

People who get discouraged are usually thinking of themselves too much. Solving any problem begins by facing it head on. We are professionals at avoiding the truth. Stop avoiding the issue. Face it head on, even if it includes admitting your portion of the blame. Absolute honesty and a refusal to ignore reality any longer is a good place to begin.

Caution: Don't become so caught up in management responsibilities that you become unthoughtful—or ungrateful—to those who are the workers.

It is both frustrating and discouraging to "load-carriers" who are never recognized except to receive a new set of instructions. Whenever credit is given for a job well done, be sure the glory is shared by *all* who have contributed in the success of the project.

TEAM PRESERVATION

A leader is of no use without people to lead. Rough and unthoughtful leadership will cause people—good people—to slip quietly away. When a leader runs, like a bulldozer, over the people he works with, the people will become weary and back off—or quit. You may win an argument and lose a worker. You may achieve your objectives but destroy your team. Retain a sensitivity to the needs of your co-workers. Travel at a reasonable pace and prevent "burn out."

Learn to trust ongoing tasks to others who are more adept and better qualified than those at the top. Decentralization strengthens top management. The broader the base, the better foundation to support the load.

DISCERNMENT

Discernment is a necessity for a leader. If you do not have it, ask for it. The sixth sense is—a must. Look again. Read between the lines.

How to know the difference between fact and rumor: a rumor source is never quoted; it is usually exaggerated and is rarely ever accurate. Most rumors are designed to hurt. Beware of the rumor mill!

I have come to the conclusion that the number one enemy of God's work is the "tongue". . .not drink, drugs, or T.V. (See the following message.)

THE SNAKE THAT POISONS EVERYBODY

It
topples
governments
wrecks
marriages,
ruins
careers,
busts
reputations,
causes
heartaches,
nightmares,
indigestion,
spawns suspicion,
generates
grief,
dispatches
innocent
people
to cry in their
pillows.
Even its name
hisses.
It's called
gossip.
Office gossip.
Shop gossip.
Party gossip.
It makes
headlines
and headaches.
Before
you repeat
a story,
ask yourself:
Is it true?
Is it fair?
Is it necessary?
If not,
shut up.

Guard against losing sight of the goal. All the "means" must lead to an "end." Administration within itself can become a bureaucratic tangle and a burden on the backs of overworked saints. The total picture should be kept in view, not the personal ambitions of a few. Every procedure must have a purpose. "Busy work" has no place in the network of the church. The structure of administration should provide the people a place to function purposefully in God's kingdom.

Don't forget the low guy on the totem pole! A pastor, superintendent, or departmental director would have a hard time carrying the load if everyone below them dropped out of sight.

SOURCE OF AUTHORITY

Christian leadership must take its cue from the Bible. It is the only acceptable source of authority by which the definition and function of Christian leadership can be determined.

Remember: the human experience is not the measuring rod of eternal truths.

BIBLICAL EXAMPLES

Moses possessed all natural and educable attributes desirable in effective leadership. He grew up in Pharoah's court and was in the line to be the heir of the throne. God reached down, snatched him from royalties of the palace, and thrust him by divine sovereignty into a position he did not want. His leadership qualities included: singleness of purpose, organizational ability, faith, obedience, and faithfulness in service. He was able to gather around him the elders of Israel who had been in Egypt many years, ignite a fire in the heart of these people, convince them that God was bent on their deliverance, and cause them to *follow* him out of Egypt. That is leadership!

Joshua. The characteristics of Godly leadership were resident in Joshua.

a. He was called to his task and was not seeking to advance himself in the ranks.
b. He had been around a long time and had held various subordinate positions of authority, without indication that he was after Moses' position.
c. He paid the price for preparation under Moses.
d. He placed a definite emphasis on courage.
e. His orders came *not* from his own ability and creativity, but a higher source—God.

Paul—tenacity of mind and conviction of belief were the marks of apostolic leadership. He knew his message (although he was offensive to many); was a man of deep affection; and yet, he had a genius for friendship.

THE DYNAMICS OF SPIRITUAL LEADERSHIP

a. Christian leadership ought to be characterized by all the legitimate earmarks of effective secular leadership, *plus* all the factors which make it distinctively Christian (faith, prayer, reality of the Holy Ghost, operations of the gifts of the Spirit), and absolute authority of God's inerrant Word as a basis for all decisions and reactions.
b. Acceptance of responsibility is the basic discipline of

all leadership. Strive to earn a reputation of faithfulness.

c. Meekness and humility: knowing that when we have done all that we could have done, we have done an excellent job; when all trophies have been received, we are still an unworthy and unprofitable servant. We cannot indulge ourselves in self-pity or dislike for others. We must minimize personality conflicts and allow the Holy Spirit to work out an attitude of meekness toward others.

   Our pattern, the Word of God, gives countless examples. Moses disciplined himself to listen for complaints. Daniel laid power and prestige on the line. Paul renounced himself continually.

d. Teachableness: the teacher who ceases to learn ceases to teach. (See Psalm 25.)

e. Care for his followers: aggressive committment to their welfare, motivated by faith.

BUREAUCRACY AND BIBLICAL LEADERSHIP

Bureaucracy is a misunderstood word. We think it to be some horrible specter of control and use it to speak out against something that is too big for us to understand, much less handle. The bureaucracy is not the problem, it is the misuse and abuse of it that is the problem. It is a *necessary tool* of productivity.

A bureaucracy is a type of organization necessary to accomplish large scale tasks by systematically coordinating the work of many individuals. A church ministry of any size must submit to the organization of a system in order to be effective.

STUDY BREAK: Make a list of situations in your Sunday school that might be resolved through better team relationships. What are the procedures that could be implemented to *begin* an improvement of the effective organization of your Sunday school?

POINTS WORTH REMEMBERING

Being a Leader

Being a leader is often thought of as a glorious and glamorous position. A more realistic appraisal is that it is, too often, an unenviable calling, more lonely and thankless than exalting. Beneath a thin veneer of publicity there can be internal strife and organizational confusion. In the following text, I would like to address *you,* the LEADER.

Are You A Leader?

Take the simple test. Look behind you. Is anyone following? The appointment to a position, *at any level,* does not automatically endue you with power and wisdom. Quite the contrary! The best leaders are servants. Leadership is influence. You will lead someone only to the measure you are able to influence them.

A good leader is highly motivated. He has a clear recognition of needs. So many leaders seem never to see the problems they ought to be solving. Individuals who have a high level of responsibility must learn to relate at the problem level. They must learn to face issues and ask hard *second questions.* They strike a balance between seeing the good things and facing reality:

PROBLEMS: Problems usually start and fester at another level but if left unresolved they will rise to meet you.

Go beyond the problem. Become personally concerned with the need. The mark of a serious leader is that he will go to God *first* with the problem. The Old Testament prophet was called upon to build the walls, but *first* he wept over the problem. This is first class compassion.

THOUGHTS AND ATTITUDES FOR LEADERSHIP

Those who aspire to leadership among God's people should develop the following attitudes:

1. Accept your own limitation.
2. Learn to lean on God. PRAY.
3. Organize an acceptable plan of action.
4. Persevere—undeterred by opposition, knowing God will finish a work *He* has begun.
5. Remember: The presence of faith does not mean the absence of organization.
6. Identify with problems—"we"—"us"—do not alienate your workers. There are no Pharoahs and slaves in this work.
7. After the problem has been identified, offer a *reasonable solution* along with a good reason for doing it that way.
8. When in conflict with another person, accept your part of the blame. There are two reasons:
   a. It is the honest thing for you to do.

b. It will disarm the adversary.

9. Be ever mindful that as a leader, you too, have superiors. Most areas of our lives come equipped with a superior—or an authority figure. God's work is not an exclusion of that rule.
10. Communication: present everything in practical facts. These facts are the foundation upon which other things are built.
11. Use orderly thinking, then transmit those thoughts via practical facts. Co-workers cannot read your mind. Nebulous thoughts which have no structure or purpose waste workers' energy and time.
12. Beware of the materialistic trap: awards and incentives that appeal to the materialistic side of workers will train them to respond to those things rather than more lasting spiritual values.
13. Before a project is attempted, take inventory.
    STEP ONE: Evaluation!
    STEP TWO: Reconstruction.
    STEP THREE: Perseverance.
14. New ideas seem to go through three channels:
    a. Rejection ("won't work!")
    b. Toleration ("O.K. as long as. . .")
    c. Acceptance ("WOW! Why didn't I think of that?")
15. Avoid three tragic mistakes often made by leadership:
    a. Aloofness—("Hey, you *down* there!")
    b. Detachment—("You!", never *"We."*)
    c. Casting blame: criticism will squelch motivation.
16. Learn to handle criticism, evaluate its origin and determine if it is valid.
17. Recognize the fragility of earthen vessels. Insensitivity to subordinates alienates you from them.

18. Approach changes in an organization cautiously. Give serious consideration to those who have worked faithfully many years. Often, inflexible persons resist change because they feel threatened.
19. Don't overlook the "bird of a feather" theory. It is true, critics will migrate to critics, the stronger swallowing up the weaker to strengthen his position.
20. Keep your eyes on the Lord. While David's brethren stood around and shuddered at the potential for loss in view of the enemy, David said, "I'll fight the giant!" He was moved by the knowledge of what could be gained by meeting the challenge at hand. "Is there not a cause?"

There are four levels of initiative (The first is every leader's dream.):

1. The person who acts and reports.
2. The person who asks what to do.
3. The person who stands around and waits to be told what to do.
4. The person who gets lost when there is work to be done.

SEVEN POINTS IN GOOD MANAGEMENT

1. List your daily responsibilities.
2. Establish your priorities.
3. Delegate whenever appropriate.
4. Develop the people under you.
5. Discover their strengths.
6. Help them solve their problems.
7. Do it NOW!

Chapter 3

Leading and Following

In the vast arena of communication, leading and following seems to be the spot where all Christians meet. It is where the war games are played. It is the playhouse where Christians either develop character or forfeit it.

In the process of leading—or following—communication isn't necessarily verbal or written. Occasionally silence, refraining from discussion of a subject, is the most rare and valuable form of communication.

Forgiveness, for example, is not communicated by words, "I forgive." It is communicated by the absence of reference to the act that required forgiveness. Learn when it is right to cease to discuss a matter.

"Picking scabs off wounds" is not one of my favorite pastimes. On the contrary, I am normally repulsed by that kind of thing. If healing is happening, leave well enough alone. Don't tamper with the cast on a fractured leg; don't change the prescription if the headache is leaving. Don't keep harping on an issue or conflict that has been resolved. Let it be! If you really want to get beyond your grief, you can't afford to keep visiting the graveyard after the funeral.

Occasionally some of these rules have to be broken. If the bone is not mending properly, it is necessary to reset the thing! Even the dead must be exhumed when essential evidence is connected with the corpse.

And so—for only a few moments I invite you to return with me to a scene all of us would rather forget. A cult compound in the steamy jungle of Guyana—Jonestown. Atrocities far more horrible and extensive than have transpired in recent history. . .but more than horrible, it was pathetic! Madmen have thrown the switch leading to the death of thousands, militia have massacred hundreds in recent years. But never in my lifetime do I recall victims volunteering to drink poison, to feed it to their own children, to lie down without a fight (in rows, if you please!) and to die face down, "looking like full grown rag dolls," as one eyewitness later reported.

Death I can accept. But one this bizarre, this meticulously choreographed, this blindly followed, I can hardly imagine. We all played follow the leader as kids. But even then when the guide in front was too daring or foolish, we would step aside. There were definite limits. But here lived 910 people, mostly adults, some full family units, over whom their leader had limitless control. They were loyal to such ultimate extremes, he was free to devise, promote, rehearse, and finally carry out a paranoid suicide pact in broad daylight with virtually no restraint. And when the whole truth was disclosed, we all learned that the man had gone beyond the bounds of propriety and trust in his personal life. Except for a few defectors, the dictator was willingly supported in spite of his prejudice, mismanagement of money, brutality, sexual perversion and open blasphemy!

No one ever defined the "follow-no-matter-what" syndrome better than our Lord in Matthew 15:14. "Let them alone: they be blind guides of the blind. And if the blind leads the blind, both shall fall into a pit!"—A PIT!

Now, let's not toss out the baby with the bath water! An inappropriate reaction to the People's carnage would be to say "all strong leaders are suspect," to clip the wings of every visionary. Remember now, Jesus warned us against *blind* guides, not *all* guides.

God still uses strategic, trustworthy, dedicated people as leaders. Always has, always will. Many guides have 20/20 vision! They walk with God. They hear from God.

But how can you tell when blindness sets in? What are the symptoms to look for in strong, natural leaders that will tell you trouble is brewing? When should you stop following lest you too become blind?

There are six blindspots to watch for:

Authoritarianism

Take care when the leader begins to suppress your freedom. When he or she becomes inflexible, dictatorial, tyrannical, and oppressive—stop following. Observe how he treats others. Does he have a servant's heart? If a teachable spirit is absent, pride is in control.

Exclusiveness

Watch out for the "us four and no more" attitude. When what is being promoted starts making you clannish, closed, cliquish, beware! This will reveal itself in an encouragement to break communications with your mate, family members, and long standing friends. Paranoia often accompanies this exclusiveness.

Greed

Money-grabbing is another tell-tale sign. Pay close attention to the leader's financial philosophy.

Sensuality

Moral purity is a must if a leader claims God's hand is on his life. Compromises in this area lead to consequences too severe to overlook. Follow no one, guru or otherwise, no matter how visionary or charismatic, who promotes and practices sexual looseness, who is too familiar with the opposite sex, who laughs at lust and flirts with infidelity. "Free love" has no place in the Kingdom of God.

Accountability

Leaders who refuse to be accountable to anyone forfeit the right to be trusted and followed. Beware of the secretive, irresponsible, untouchable "I am God's annointed" mentality. No matter how eloquent or how competent, no one can sufficiently maintain a leadership role without counsel and an occasional confrontation.

Rationalization

When wrong is justified with a defensive spirit, when inappropriate actions are quickly glossed over, when scriptural truth is twisted to fit a sinful life style, when grey-black facts are whitewashed, *stop your support.* Look for a sensitive conscience, a quick willingness to admit wrong in the one you follow. More important than the act is the spirit of the individual when the sin is discovered.

Following a leader who is reliable and maintains your trust is both challenging and rewarding. But existing under the hypnotic, demanding spell of prima donna, is exactly as Jesus described in Matthew 15:14. . .THE PITS!

Take His advice—"Let them alone."

GENERAL NOTES:

* Leading and following is the heartbeat of all communication. You will at all times be doing one or the other. You will never rise to such a height that you will cease to follow.

* If subjection, submission, and forfeiting your own opinion is a problem, you better learn to pray. This type of spirit will cause you problems—you will go out of one problem into another.

* There are ways to deal with problems. Learn them. Learn to maintain:

1. sensitivity
2. temper
3. emotional equilibrium

* Pastoral leadership requires three things:

1. compassion
2. servant spirit
3. teachable spirit

FOOTNOTES

Charles Swindoll, *Make Up Your Mind About The Issues of Life,* Multnomah Press, 1981, p. 58, 59.

Reflections On Self Image

Chapter 4

Life

I am going to use the Word of God to speak to you from my heart and I believe that God will use me, hopefully, to speak to you from His heart. I would like to talk to you about Life. I feel very concerned about several areas and I feel the Lord has been speaking to me about some things and I would like to deliver those to you.

I am going to ask you to turn to the 12th chapter of Luke. The 12th chapter of Luke I have come to call the "life" chapter because from this Scripture I have seen and heard the voice of the Lord Jesus as He spoke to me relative to my life and how I can come into a new philosophy, better than my own, in knowing how to deal with several things—how to cope with several areas.

Recently I have become extremely concerned as I view the dilemma in which I find many people as they face life. I have not always stood at vantage points such as where I stand today, by virtue of the fact that I was young and now I am getting older. There are certain things that you do not see, nor comprehend, until after a certain number of years have passed in your life. I wish it were not so; I wish that I could have had the opportunity to see things and feel certain things many years ago that I feel and see today. I did the next best thing. I took the word of my parents and my minister friends, those who were fathers in the Lord to me, many of whom I would not begin to name because the list is more than one or two, people that I have revered, people that I have looked up to. People that I have listened to. These people I watched and tried to reap from them and from their ministry in certain times, areas and facets of wisdom, thereby saving myself many heartaches, heartbreaks and frustrations.

I would admonish every college student, every young mother, every person reading this book, every head of every household, that if you can find a good example, if you can discern certain words of wisdom, write it down. Read it often. Set aside your own opinions. Listen to the wise counsel of other people and in so doing you will save yourself from making mistakes and your life will be richer.

Let's read from Luke chapter 12:

> *"In the mean time, when there are gathered together an innumerable multitude of people, insomuch that they trode one upon another, he began to say unto his disciples first of all, Beware ye of the leaven of the Pharisees, which is hypocrisy. For there is nothing covered, that shall not be revealed; neither hid, that shall not be known. Therefore whatsoever ye have spoken in darkness shall be heard in the light; and that which ye have spoken in the ear in closets shall be proclaimed upon the house tops. And I say unto you my friends, Be not afraid of them that kill the body, and after that have no more that they can*

do. But I will forewarn you whom ye shall fear; Fear him, which after he hath killed hath power to cast into hell; yea, I say unto you, Fear him. Are not five sparrows sold for two farthings, and not one of them is forgotten before God? But even the very hairs of your head are all numbered. Fear not therefore: ye are of more value than many sparrows. Also I say unto you, Whosoever shall confess me before men, him shall the Son of man also confess before the angels of God: But he that denieth me, before men shall be denied before the angels of God. And whosoever shall speak a word against the Son of man, it shall be forgiven him: but unto him that blasphemeth against the Holy Ghost it shall not be forgiven. And when they bring you unto the synagogues, and unto magistrates, and powers, take ye no thought how or what thing ye shall answer, or what ye shall say: For the Holy Ghost shall teach you in the same hour what ye ought to say. And one of the company said unto him, Master, speak to my brother, that he divide the inheritance with me. And he said unto him, Man, who made me a judge or a divider over you?"

I want you to notice how that Jesus is laying down some ground rules for living in this life. He is expressing some profound concepts relative to philosophy.

"And he said unto them, Take heed, and beware of covetousness: for a man's life consisteth not in the abundance of the things which he possesseth. And he spake a parable unto them, saying, The ground

of a certain rich man brought forth plentifully: And he thought within himself, saying, What shall I do, because I have no room where to bestow my fruits? And he said, This will I do: I will pull down my barns, and build greater; and there will I bestow all my fruits and my goods. And I will say to my soul, Soul, thou hast much goods laid up for many years; take thine ease, eat, drink, and be merry. But God said unto him, Thou fool, this night thy soul shall be required of thee: then whose shall those things be, which thou hast provided? So is he that layeth up treasure for himself, and is not rich toward God. And he said unto his disciples, Therefore I say unto you, Take no thought for your life, what ye shall eat; neither for the body, what ye shall put on. The life is more than meat, and the body is more than raiment. Consider the ravens; for they neither sow nor reap; which neither have storehouse nor barn; and God feedeth them: how much more are ye better than the fowls? And which of you with taking thought can add to his stature one cubit? If ye then be not able to do that thing which is least, why take ye thought for the rest?"

Jesus addresses the problem of anxiety about Life—

"Consider the lilies how they grow: they toil not, they spin not; and yet I say unto you, that Solomon in all his glory was not arrayed like one of these. If then God so clothe the grass, which is to day in the field, and to morrow is cast into the oven; how much more will he clothe you, O ye of little faith?"

He's addressing another problem:

> *"And seek not ye what ye shall eat, or what ye shall drink. . ."*

Notice He did not say, "*whether* ye shall eat or *whether* ye shall drink." The word "what" is used there. It refers to an overdose of concern about the nature of life, the quality of life, or anxiety about how things are going to be. "Take no thought what ye shall eat or what ye shall drink."

Then He addressed another problem I'd like to talk with you about,

> *"Neither be ye of doubtful mind."*

That is pessimism; that is negativity; that is worrying; that is fretting.

> *"For all these things do the nations of the world seek after."*

In other words, pessimism, worrying, fretting, negativity are attributes of the world. They are concerned about the Joneses, not knowing that as soon as they catch up with them they will refinance and start all over again. Jesus said:

> *"Your Father knoweth that ye have need of these things. But rather seek ye the kingdom of God; and all these things shall be added unto you."*

Here He, in this next verse, hits head-on with a Life problem.

"Fear not, little flock; for it is your Father's good pleasure to give you the kingdom. Sell that ye have, and give alms; provide yourselves bags which wax not old, a treasure in the heavens that faileth not, where no thief approacheth, neither moth corrupteth."

Here is a foundation stone; here is something you can hitch your wagon to.

"For where your treasure is, there will your heart be also."

Now, He issues straightforward command remedies for the problem. I love it when Jesus just starts taking the hammer and hitting the nail on the head!

"Let your loins be girded about, and your lights burning; And ye yourselves like unto men that wait for their lord, when he will return from the wedding; that when he cometh and knocketh, they may open unto him immediately. Blessed are those servants, whom the lord when he cometh shall find watching: verily I say unto you that he shall gird himself, and make them to sit down to meat, and will come forth and serve them. And if he shall come in the second watch, or come in the third watch, and find them so, blessed are those servants. And this know, that if the goodman of the house had known what hour the thief would come, he would have watched, and not have suffered his house to be broken through. Be ye therefore ready also: for

the Son of man cometh at an hour when ye think not. Then Peter said unto him, Lord, speakest thou this parable unto us, or even to all?"

Is this a message for His chosen few or is this general information for everyone?

"And the Lord said, Who then is that faithful and wise steward, whom his lord shall make ruler over his household, to give them their portion of meat in due season? Blessed is that servant."

I love the way Jesus makes people answer their own questions.

"Blessed is that servant, whom his lord when he cometh shall find so doing. Of a truth I say unto you, that he will make him ruler over all that he hath. But and if that servant say in his heart, My lord delayeth his coming; and shall begin to beat the menservants and maidens, and to eat and drink, and to be drunken; The lord of that servant will come in a day when he looketh not for him, and at an hour when he is not aware, and will cut him in sunder, and will appoint him his portion with the unbelievers. And that servant, which knew his lord's will, and prepared not himself, neither did according to his will, shall be beaten with many stripes. But he that knew not, and did commit things worthy of stripes, shall be beaten with few stripes. For unto whomsoever much is given, of him shall be much required: and to whom men have committed much, of him

they will ask the more. I am come to send fire on the earth; and what will I, if it be already kindled? But I have a baptism to be baptized with; and how am I straitened till it be accomplished! Suppose ye that I am come to give peace on earth? I tell you, Nay; but rather division.''

And so on and so on. *Life.*

Let's note that the rich fool confused life with eternity and eternity with life. I want you to notice that after he had gained certain gain and had made it very comfortable for himself, he then became confused between life and eternity and made one tragic mistake. The mistake was not in the accumulation of goods. The mistake was not in what he had. The mistake was not in the size of the barns nor the quantity that filled them. The mistake was when he confused what was for this life and what was for the life to come, what was for here and now and what was for the soul. He was mistaken when he believed that the barns and the things that filled them could satisfy the soul. For he said ''I will build greater barns then I will say, soul. . .'' He should have said ''Jack'' or ''John'' or ''Greg'' or ''Ron.'' He should have said, ''Ron, take thine ease.'' You see that is the body. But his mistake was that he confused those things relative to *life* with things relative to the *soul,* and you have to keep those things in perspective.

I do not believe that God cares how much you have as long as you keep things in perspective. I don't believe God minds for a moment how many stocks and bonds you have laid up as long as you don't make the mistake of believing that they will satisfy the soul, as long as you don't neglect the soul. So the man said, ''soul take thine ease, eat, drink and be merry." Souls can't eat barns; souls can't eat grain; souls can't wear clothes; souls can't drive cars; souls don't work jobs, bodies do. Bodies wear clothes, bodies work jobs, bodies eat food—but not souls. We have to keep eternal things (spiritual things, that is) and natural things in perspective.

He thought he was providing for his soul when he was actually only providing for his body, and the possession of those things at his death ended because Jesus posed the question, "Whose then will these things be?" In verse 22, Jesus said, "Be not anxious for your life, what ye shall eat (not *whether* ye shall eat, but *what* ye shall eat) and for the body (not *whether* ye shall have a cloak to put on, but the anxiety comes in the color of the cloak, the style of the cloak, whether or not it is new or old; this is anxiousness about Life)."

We live in a changing world. Social structures have changed rapidly; they are changing. There are, for example, more women in the work force today than ever before and this is changing even more rapidly.

Brother Trout and I see problems in our office that are a result of the changing social structure of American culture. You are being victimized by the rapid pace in which things are changing and many of the life-frustrations that you are experiencing today are a result of the socio-economic situation in America. The two-job, three-job syndrome, the making bills and having to get more jobs to pay more bills to get more money to spend on more things that bring more bills that demand more jobs. That is the vicious cycle you live in.

Let's take a poll that will be very interesting I'm sure. I am going to ask every woman in this room that works on a public job or works out of the home to lift your hand. Take a look around. Now, conversely, how many of you do not work on a job? You stay at home. Would you lift your hand? You are in the minority. As a result of this syndrome, role changing has transpired in our society and many anxieties are being imposed on people.

Today I wish to address some of these areas. I have prayed to God that I will be able to help you. I am certain that this chapter is not going to cause you to shout. I feel fairly confident that this chapter may not leave you weeping. Perhaps it will. Who knows what will happen? However, I don't foresee the nature of this chapter causing you to want to get up and run around the room and expend your spiritual energy. I am very deeply distressed about some things that I see happening in people and with people. I feel frustrated in my heart, and as a result of that frustration I have asked God to give me something to give you to help stabilize you if you are one of those individuals who feel confused about life and the priorities on how to deal with certain emotions that are taking place within you today. As we experience changes in our culture and as things transpire rapidly around us, do not get caught up in the syndromes and be victimized by them.

Sometimes you can be half way to where you thought you were going only to find you were following the wrong leader. You can become frustrated when you suddenly realize that you were patterning your life after someone who really did not have everything that you thought they had. Examples and models are a wonderful thing, but they are also a very hazardous route to follow.

There was a fellow who came by the clock shop everyday, I am told, and pulled his pocket watch out of his pocket, flipped it open, and set his watch by the clock that was in the shop window. Everyday the owner of the clock shop would watch him do this and finally one day he decided, "I ought to go out and meet this fellow who comes everyday and sets his pocket watch by my clock. I think I am honored that he would do this." So, after watching him for many weeks, he decided to go out one day and say hello to him. He went out and said, "Hi, I am the owner of the clock shop and I've been watching you. Everyday you come by my shop, stop and pull out your watch and set it by my clock. I just wanted to come out and meet you. I'm really proud that you would do a thing like that. By the way," he said, "where do you work?" And the man said, "I work at the factory just down the street." The clock owner said, "What do you do?" The man said, "Well, I blow the whistle everyday at 12:00 noon." And the owner of the shop stopped and his face dropped, he became very serious and he said, "We have a problem my friend. I set the clock by that whistle every day."

So much of what we are and what we do, how we respond and how we dress, how we walk, how we comb our hair, and the list goes on, is a result of what we see other people do. We need to be careful in this area. God is calling for people who seek His face independently and establish themselves firmly upon concepts that are Bible founded. We want to be an amalgamation of people who have singularly sought God and have obtained for themselves from the throne of God personal convictions that are solid and Bible centered, things that will stick to your ribs, and that will straighten your life out, that will give you philosophies and concepts that will give you faith and remove doubts and fears. It will give you direction and remove the anxiety about the things that you do everyday. If you can do this, you will remove from your whole atmosphere, from your personality, and your job situation, anxieties that are now causing your problem.

So much of what we are and what we do is a result of what someone else has pulled down from God for us. If we could ever lay hold on our full potential singularly without worrying about who's called what, who gets the credit, what kind of titles are worn or positions are held.

It's not so much what we *have* that matters; it is what we *do* with what we have that matters. The media is a good example of that. I was, for a number of years, in the radio station at 6:00 in the morning. I stood in the teletype room and watched the news as it came across the teletype machine. It has become very clear to me that it is not the news that gains ABC a first rating across the country. Actually ABC has the same access to news that CBS or NBC has, but it is what they *do* with what they *have.* All of those other fellows don't have a Walter Cronkite. But they're catching on and now the term "anchor man" is becoming synonymous with the number one rating. Everyone else feels like they have to have an anchor man. Yet they all get the same information. Walter doesn't make the news, he doesn't write the news, Walter just reads the news. It's not what he has that makes him what he is, but it's what he does with what he has that makes him what he is and earns him what he gets.

Somebody is feeling all "down in the mouth" because someone else seems to excel or to be, quote, "used more than someone else." That's not it, my friend. You are on a pity party! Why do some make it and some do not make it? It's the different life within the individual. God gives everybody an equal portion. Then there are those who are especially gifted; but Jesus said that to whom much is given, much is required. And so we are still back to base number one. We are still equal. So if you didn't get much, He doesn't require much of you. So you are still ahead of the game. It's not what you have that matters. It's what you *do* with what you *have* that matters.

There are some people that can make it regardless of the circumstances. I've seen people who could sell ice to an Eskimo! It's the truth! I heard about the man who sold hearing aids. He said to the fellow, "What do you do for a living?" The gentleman said, "I sell hearing aids." The fellow said, "Really, how much are they?" The salesman said, "I can sell you a hearing aid anywhere from $2.50 to $2,500.00." The guy said, "$2,500.00 is a little steep. Let me see the $2.50 one." So he pulled out of his pocket a button with a string tied on it. The salesman said, "That's a hearing aid. You put the button in your ear and the string in your pocket and people talk louder."

The battlefield of this hour in which we live is human relations—people getting along with people. Now I am getting down in the cuticle. I am coming down to where you live. Human beings dealing with human beings. Everyone of us could improve in this area. There are ways that this improvement can occur if we can get our act together. I believe that if a person can devote the attention to it that is deserved, that is needed, then he can become an expert in human relations.

Have you ever seen one of these individuals who can get along with anybody and that everybody likes? Oh, to be one of those; unfortunately, that boat I missed.

But we can *become* one of those people with a lot of

study, effort, and with a lot of prayer. It's called personality adjustments or—*prayer meeting.* You can't come out of a prayer meeting and bawl somebody out. You can't come out of a prayer meeting and lose your temper. You can't come out of a prayer meeting and kick the dog half way across the yard. Prayer meeting, called "personality adjustment," is where everything is neutralized. All the acid is neutralized in the prayer room. So one of the first steps to learn in human relations is to learn how to pray.

Prayer will also help your self-image. You do not think as highly of yourself as you ought to think in many instances. I am aware of the fact that the Scripture warns us against thinking more highly of ourselves than we ought, but I don't really think that is a problem. With most people self-image is the more likely problem. Most of us don't think as highly of ourselves as we ought to think.

There is a U.S. Government study which says 75% of Americans are neurotic. So look around—if you see three or four other people or so that are in good shape, then you are in trouble! You're the one that's the neurotic! Self-image—most of us have a problem in that area. Too big, too fat, too tall, too short, too white, too black, doesn't look this, doesn't look that, the most important statement you can make to yourself in your whole lifetime is "I am." Amen. "I am."

There are a lot of publications on the market today about awareness and I am not getting into that area. Some of that is very dangerous. You need to be selective when you read that kind of information. What you need to know is what you have got going for yourself. You need to become aware of your good points and not constantly and eternally put yourself down. You have the capabilities of doing some things and doing them very well. You just need somebody to help you recognize that. Let me pay you a compliment and tell you that I think you're pretty nice. After all, you are reading this book.

There is a story about a fellow who worked in a Communist factory and everyday he went through the factory gate pushing a wheelbarrow full of straw. The guard looked through the straw and when he did not find anything he let him go. The second day the worker came through the gate pushing a wheelbarrow full of straw. The guard searched the straw thoroughly, didn't find anything, and so he let him go. The third day he came through the gate pushing a wheelbarrow full of straw. The guard searched the straw thoroughly and still couldn't find anything and finally he said, "Fellow, I'm being transferred to another place and I'd just like to ask you one question because I probably won't see you again here. I'd like to know what's going on. I know you're stealing but I can't figure it out. What are you stealing?" The fellow answered, "Wheelbarrows." Lesson: All of us do something well!

The first thing you need to do is pay a compliment to yourself. Get accustomed to thinking more highly of yourself. Get to know yourself a little better. We look at ourselves at a great distance sometimes because we do not like to see ourselves close up. We don't like what we see when we look closely. So you need a better self-image. Sometimes our self-image is a result of truth and so if that is a problem get after it, do something about it. If you think you are too fat, go on a diet. What's wrong with that? If you think you're ugly, go to somebody and ask them to help you fix yourself up. Maybe you are wearing the wrong color. Maybe you're wearing the wrong size for yourself.

Maybe you parted your hair on the wrong side. I don't know, but you can find out. Sometimes our self-image is viewed through truth of things about which we can do something. How many years have you gone through life suffering the blows you give yourself every day when in fact if you stop analyzing, sit up and take notice, do something about it, correct it, you will feel better about yourself.

Stop knocking each other and learn to work together. God has given us a beautiful network here. You may feel that you have good ideas. But you may feel that nobody is paying attention, then that causes your self-image to drop. You may suffer from that. When you feel like that you're not important, that can be a problem.

I heard about the little boy who joined the little league and he came home and he said to his dad, "Dad, I got traded." And his dad said, "That's okay, son. People get traded in baseball." He said, "Reggie Jackson got traded, Pete Rose got traded, Babe Ruth got traded. That's not unusual." The kid said, "But Dad, you don't understand, I got traded for a glove." Now that can make you feel kind of little and unimportant.

There comes that day when we feel that nobody is paying any attention to us. The worst thing in the world is not to be interrupted but the worst thing in the world is to be ignored. Sometimes that really hurts.

Parents, don't ignore your children. You can be about them and around them every day but essentially still be ignoring them.

When learning to cope with life situations you learn to cope with other people's thoughts and opinions. There are some people who are so neurotic about adversaries they become absolutely distraught with opposing opinion. You need to learn to cope with the thought that somebody else may have a better idea. In every group, there is somebody who is the smartest person and then there is somebody who is the dumbest. There are all kinds of persons and that can be hard to cope with. It's hard to cope with uncertain people. Maturity is measured by the degree of pain or exhilaration that you feel when you are confronted with a new idea—with an opposing opinion.

Human relations! Getting along in life. Learning that life is more than what you eat. Life is more than what you wear. You live life twenty-four hours a day. I want to help you have a quality existence. There is nothing that makes me more sad than seeing a person who is miserable everyday, all day long, about everything and everybody. I tell you the honest truth my friend, you are reading about one lady who would not live that way. I would kick, scratch, crawl, scream, shout, fight, dig out, throw away until I found out what the problem was and then I would stand there and chew it to death until my teeth wore out and then I would beat it with my gums. That is how I feel about being miserable every day.

I love living and I love feeling good and I love being happy and I love getting along with other people and I love reaching out for people and helping people. I love it and I don't understand these people who live day in and day out, week in and week out, month in and month out, year in and year out, a whole lifetime some of them live, and never smile, never laugh, never enjoy anything or anybody. I tell you if that is what you enjoy, you have it by yourself but you keep it a country mile away from me. Because I like to laugh, I like to love, I like to reach out, I like to touch,

I like to hug, I like to have a great time. I like to feel good in my heart, not just about my soul, not just about my eternity, not just about rapture and the Lord and salvation and redemption. All of those things have a tremendous bearing upon the way I feel. I'm talking about everyday living. If you are miserable most of the time, there is a problem. And you need to go to work on it and "gum it" to death.

You learn not to be manipulated nor manipulate as you live this life. You learn to manage your affairs rather than have your affairs manage you. That could be part of the problem. You learn to take charge and do something about the things that are causing confusion.

Now I am not ignorant of the fact that many people are victims of circumstances over which they have no control. However, I have seen classic examples in my lifetime of people who learn how to be victorious within themselves, even though they have to live in a hell on earth everyday. I say it can be done and as long as you are not dead there is hope. You will not always be able to change everything to suit yourself but you can meet God in a prayer room frequently and you can have an awareness and a perspective on life that will bring to the darkened and dingy shadows of your soul, your being and your mind a cool refreshing breeze from the presence of the Lord that will provide for you inner peace regardless of the circumstances. Did He not promise that He would give you peace that passes all understanding? God, by His spirit, can do that for you if you will just hang on, hold on, keep on, keep working, keep trying. You can do it!

Let's think about manipulation. Children manipulate their parents. Parents are manipulated by children because they let it happen. I am sure that if the stage is set it is going to be hard to change the props by now, but it is worth a try. Give it a whirl. You might be so pleased with the results that you will keep it up, but don't be manipulated and, of all things, don't be manipulative. AMEN!

There was a young man who joined the army and he went down for his physical and he was called in before the psychiatrist. The psychiatrist said, "Young man, I guess you know you are going to be going into the army."

He grinned a little bit and he said, "Yeah, doc, I think it's great, I've been looking forward to it. I've been reading all my life about the army and I can't wait to get into the army. It's a wonderful thing to do with my life."

"Young man, you may have to travel overseas," the doctor continued.

"Travel, do you mean they've thrown in travel in this bargain? That's great. Where do you suppose I'll be going? All around the world?" He asked excitedly.

"Young man, you don't understand something. You may have to take up weapons," the doctor went on.

"Weapons, do you think they'll give me a cannon? If I could get a cannon, what I couldn't do."

"Hey fellow, you still don't understand. They may put a bayonet in your hand."

"Bayonet!" And his eyes began to dance. "Just think, doc, I can ram that bayonet through them. I can pin them to the wall. There will be blood and guts all over the place."

"Young man, you are crazy," the doctor concluded.

"Write it down, doc, write it down," the young man insisted.

Manipulated—be careful. Be careful.

We must also learn to deal with conflict. Learn to solve problems, not symptoms. Young mothers ignorantly bounce a baby on her knee for thirty minutes trying to get it to stop crying and with every bounce it goes, squish, squish, squish, and the poor darling does not know that all the little sweetheart wants is its diaper changed.

If in this life we could learn to deal with the problem and not the symptom. We spend most of our time and most of our frustration, anger and irritation on symptoms instead of problems. The symptom is the crying, the problem is the wet diaper. The symptom is the screaming, the problem is the pin that's sticking. I've had young mothers bring their screaming babies to me and say to me, "I've done everything." The first thing I do is sit down, lay the baby across my knee, check everything about its clothes; neck too tight, waist too tight, the diaper cutting into its leg, and in his shoes his little toe is bent completely backward and here comes this mother dragging the toddler who has been screaming for two hours because its toe has been backward in its shoe. The mother has done everything but climb the wall and all she had to do was take the shoe off the baby's foot.

So much of our time is spent working on symptoms and we need to get to the problem. As a result of that, we feel *irritation, anger* and *frustration*.

There were three or four fellows sitting around the table drinking coffee very late one night. One of them was a philosopher and he said he was trying to explain to the other two the difference between irritation, anger and frustration. He said, "Give me a dime, I'll just illustrate it to you." He walked over to the telephone. (It's 2:00 a.m. in the morning). He dialed a number. The person answered, "Hello." "Is Mike there?" he asked. "Mike? There's no Mike here," replied the gentleman on the line.

Bang, he hung up the phone kind of heavy. He was irritated. The guy said to the fellows, "That's *irritation!* Give me another dime." They gave him another dime. He dialed the same number.

The fellow answered the phone. "Is Mike there?"

"Mike, there's no Mike here. If I knew where you were, I'd call the police," the man cursed him a little bit and he added, "Don't you know you've awakened me and my wife. Don't call this number again." Bang, and he hung up the phone.

The fellow said, "That's anger! Okay guys, you got that, that's *anger*. Got another dime?" They gave him another dime. He dialed the same number.

"Hello!" the man on the other end answered.

"Hi, I'm Mike, do I have any messages?" the fellow asked.

"That's *frustration.*"

The premise is this. Let's solve the problem, not the symptom. Can we do it? Yes we can. We can do it. There are three great problems that hold us back from achieving anything whether it has to do with your life, whether it has to do with your walk with God or whether it has to do with your success in a job, your marriage, your family, you name it, there are three areas that will hold you back from achieving what you need to achieve. *The number one problem is doubt.* That's that horrible feeling you get when you don't know what to do. It's a basic problem because you don't know what to do and because you don't know what to do you don't know what to do with what you don't know what to do with. It's called doubt.

Now there is a Chinese proverb that says, "Dig the well before you get thirsty." Pray before the storm comes. This means that we would not have to worry and doubt if we have listened and learned some things in the first place. But we have a way of becoming so issue-oriented that we forget good solid principles of life, of living, of human relations, of co-existing with other people. We become less than compassionate toward other individuals and extremely impatient with their lack of maturity. We get so oriented toward issues that we forget the underlying problems. I have come to believe that many people that I used to think were lazy are not lazy—they just have no direction. They don't know what to do and so *laziness is a form of despair* for them. If you think your child is lazy, stop a moment. Did you take the time to work with him and show him how to properly do what you are demanding that he do? Did you assume that he knew how to do what you asked him to do? Maybe he isn't lazy after all. Perhaps you have never taken the time to address the problem instead of the symptom.

If we are going to settle our problems and not our symptoms, we must clean up our doubt and we must fill it with faith. Believe! You've got to believe. Your mind must be brought from a state of negativity into a neutral state and from that point launch into positiveness. You can't just jump from negativity to positiveness. You have to be brought from a negative into a neutral state and from that neutral state begin to work on the positive things. So many of the problems we experience are all right here behind two eyeballs. Faith. It's not going to church to pray for rain in the time of drought. Faith is going to church in the time of drought to pray for rain and taking an umbrella with you so you won't get wet on your way home. That's faith. That's believing. That's the added dimension.

Be an optimist. Don't be a pessimist. You give yourself too much liberty in your mind. You allow yourself to think certain negative thoughts about yourself, things and others that entrap you in the state of mind that is doubtful and full of negative things which prohibits the activity of the Spirit of God.

Did not the Apostle Paul say:

> *"Whatsoever things are true, whatsoever things are honest, . . .whatsoever things are of good report, . . .think on these things" (Philippians 4:8).*

A pessimist sees the obstacle in every opportunity. An optimist sees an opportunity behind every obstacle. An optimist believes that he can eat the chicken that's scratching over his grave for Sunday dinner. An optimist believes he can make it. It is astounding how much the way we think, how we think, how we feel, is linked together with the activity of the Spirit of God in our lives. Why, honestly, I do not believe that the Holy Ghost feels at ease in the house of an individual who is perpetually downcast and downtrodden and pessimistic and negative about everything and everybody. I believe the Holy Ghost takes pleasure in walking in the life of an individual that is full of vibrancy and faith and effervescence and optimism. I believe that all of these things will improve the quality of your living because it affects the way you *are* which affects the way you affect people which changes the atmosphere in which you live and that's what we're talking about. LIFE!

Fear is another obstacle that must be surmounted. Afraid to act. This country is on "hold" because people are afraid to act. The President is afraid to act, the Congress is afraid to act. Each one is waiting for the other one to act and no one is doing anything about anything.

Fear will put your whole life on hold if you don't watch it. People are afraid to move, and with the economy like it is, it's like a bouncing ball. It just goes from one side to the other, up and down. Fear will not let you go but you must learn to let go of fear. Fear will entrap you. Fear will hold you so that the thing that is pursuing you will overtake you and capture you.

The devil is a roaring lion walking about seeking whom he may devour and the first and easiest prey are those people who permit themselves to live constantly in a state of fear. Fear will entrap you. Fear will make you hold on to some things. You just won't give them over to God, you won't turn them loose to other people.

You know how they catch monkeys in the jungle? They take a coconut, drill a hole in the top, chop the coconut up into little pieces and drop it in the hole. The monkey runs his hand in to get the coconut. He grasps it in his hand and then he can't take his hand out of the coconut because he won't let go. Then he starts running with the coconut hanging from his hand. In just a matter of time you've got him.

Some people are totally and constantly encased in a trap of fear because there are certain things they won't let go of. But then you learn to let go and let God have His way. Oh, just to relax knowing that it's all in His hands.

There is a lady in the Northeast church that has been attending for years. She smoked cigarettes. She has chain-smoked for years and years and years. Her daughters continually requested prayer for her. Finally in one Sunday morning service the Lord swept across that place with His presence as we worshiped Him at the opening of the class and she began to weep. I left the platform and went down and started to pray with her. As I did she started to weep and I told her, "Today is the day God can baptize you with the Holy Ghost, today after all of these years. He can do it today."

"Sister Trout, what about my husband, what about these cigarettes?" she asked through her tears. "Stop, take just a moment now and let's put all of that in the Lord's hands. Let them go," I instructed her.

She began to sob and say, "Oh, God, I put my husband in your hands and I know you're going to take care of it." As she began to release from her grip the things that plagued her heart, the Spirit of the Lord began to move across her and in a matter of moments she was speaking in tongues as the Spirit of God gave the utterance.

You, too, can be baptized in the Holy Ghost when you loosen your grip on things you've held on to; the fear of reprisal, the fear of envy, the fear of God and traditional religion. The old things, the old church and the list goes on. Turn it loose, my friend. Let it drop and God will take care of you.

Emerson said, "What lies behind us and what lies before us are tiny matters compared to what lies within us."

The Scripture said, "Greater is he that is within us (or you) than he that is in the world."

Then *we must learn to cope with anxiety.* The definition of the word *anxiety* is problems that have not happened yet. Eighty percent of what you are anxious about never comes to pass. We think ourselves into a problem. It's like the pastor saying to you on Friday afternoon just before you leave the building, "Brother Reed, I'd like to see you in my office first thing Monday morning." And you're going to try to have a good weekend? Oh, no. Come Monday morning Brother Trout calls him in the office and says, "Mark, I just want to tell you something and I haven't taken the time to do so. I want to take the time right now. I was so busy Friday, I was late for an appointment so I didn't stop to tell you. I think you're doing a great job." Mark thinks, "Why didn't he tell me that before I bawled Diana out. Why didn't he tell me that before I kicked the tire when I walked by my car." Anxiety!

I know a lot of people who are afraid to fly because they have thought themselves into anxiety. Look at the way they have dealt with flying, and it might help us to be a little more sympathetic toward them. You come into the airport and there is a big sign in block letters and it says PERMANENT PARKING and you ask, "What do they mean by that?" And then you get over that one. After you leave your car and haul all of your suitcases into the building, going down the concourse on the way to the plane you pass this little machine and think "I'll stop and play a game of Pac Man." Then walk over there and realize that it's Life Insurance and it hits you again and then you think "Lord, help me! I'll give it another try." You look around for signs for which way to go and finally you see one that says DEPARTURE. Anxiety! We think most of our anxieties into existence. So you will deal with anxiety by learning to deal with the *problem,* not the *symptom.*

How do we wrap all of this up? It's called 3-D, 3-D vision, *super* vision. Learning to take charge of your own affairs. Learning to square your shoulders. Learning to face life with a smile if not a grin. Learning to be victorious—not only with matters pertaining to the soul but matters pertaining to everyday life. I tell you why I am writing this chapter. I see a lot of people that come to church week after week and they hear so many sermons on spiritual things and we talk a lot about heaven but we have never seen it. We believe it's there and we believe we're going. But I have felt a real quickening in my heart that I needed to take some time with you and help you cope with the here and now. It's all right if we can talk about the never, never land, the far blue yonder, but how about the nasty here and now and about things that bother you today? What about the worries on your mind now? What about the depressed feelings you have now, what about the fears, what about the doubts, can you get over those things? I am here to tell you, "Yes you can." I am telling you that you can make it. Let's get some 3-D vision today.

First, you need *desire.* The beginning of all achievement is not a wish. It's a goal, a desire. It is something solid that will send you in long hurdles toward your goal. It must be a burning desire. You're not going to get across the Grand Canyon in short hops. You're going to look at that gapping hole and you're going to have to back up and take a running start. You're going to have to stretch those legs as long as you can get them and give it all you've got—*desire.*

I used to watch Anthony when he ran track at Kent Christian Academy as a high school student. If something would go wrong with someone's body, you would always know it was Anthony. He signed up for typing, he broke his finger. It just seemed to happen to him but there was such a desire in him to be a good athlete. Although he knew that the minute he hit the ground after the race the cramps would overtake him, that desire to win would consume him. I've seen him do that long jump and I thought that he was going to crumple into a dozen pieces and break every bone in his body. I would see the sweat pouring from his brow and he gave it everything he had and I watched him stretch those long legs and get out there and win it. I watched him run track, I saw him do the 100 yard dash and 220 yard dash, and I saw him when that ribbon was stretched across that track and he would give it that last kick on that last little lap. He gave it everything he had and his chest would break through that ribbon and he had won it again because in him was a burning desire.

I want to tell you something, friend, if you're having trouble living for God or you are just having trouble living period, you had better work on the desire mechanism in your life. That could be the root of your problem. The way God put us together we don't do much of anything that we don't really want to do and so you are going to have to work from a want-to standpoint. "Delight yourself in the Lord," the Scripture says, "and He will give you the desires of your heart."

Someone called me the other day and said, "Sister Trout, I read that Scripture and it bothers me."

"Well, what bothers you about that Scripture?"

"I am afraid that I will desire the wrong things and God will give them to me. Then what do I do?" she asked.

"Wait just a minute. The second half of the verse is revolutionized by the first half. So if the desires are wrong or if they are in error or for the wrong things, go back to the first half. Delight thyself in the Lord and when you are delighted the desires are in the Lord and there isn't any way you're going to go wrong and then He is safe in giving you the desires of your heart. The delight in the Lord completely revolutionizes your desires," I told her.

Secondly, you need *direction.* Intensity governed by illusion becomes disastrous. If you are going to be intense, please don't work in an illusionary vision. Make sure you have direction. Know what you are doing, what you're after. And you've got to know where you are going. You have to have direction. You have to know what you are looking for. You have to know what you are after.

This reminds me of the day Anthony took Tammy deer hunting with him. She wanted to go. "Honey, you won't have any fun and you will get dirty. You have to sit in a tree, you don't know how to aim the gun," he tried to discourage her.

"I want to go," she insisted.

And so he said all right. He took her into the woods and gave her a gun and put her in a tree. Then he said, "Now the first deer that comes along shoot it and when I hear the noise I'll come help you." He walked away and he left her to go to his deer stand. A few minutes later he heard bang bang. Oh no! He went running and walked up just in time to see this man with a big wide brim hat saying to her, "Okay lady, if you say it's a deer you can have it but would you let me please take the saddle off it!" You need direction if you are going to get where you are going. (That story is hypothetical, of course.)

Thirdly, you need *determination.* The beginning of every achievement is not the goal. After you get started, you've got to keep on going. I say this especially to college students. I am sure that the opportunity to lag and sag has already presented itself but in order to make it here or anywhere else you have to have determination. Find your direction. Narrow your choices. Keep your priorities in order and get after it. Go get it. Don't let your life be one continuous losing situation. Think how many years you have already wasted. Think of how many souls you could have already affected. Think of how many people you could have won to God. Think of how many Bible studies that you could have already completed and how many people could have already been baptized. Think of what could have already been done if you hadn't given up so soon. Determination! Give yourself a goal. You need a triumph. You need to know how to rejoice, work hard then give yourself a treat. Do what you *have to do* then you can do *what you want* to do.

Learn to celebrate, learn to relax, learn to breathe, give yourself a chance, sit down, enjoy, smile, don't be so hard on yourself. Don't be a slave driver. Don't be a workaholic. People say, "Sister Trout, you're a workaholic." No, I have learned to celebrate. You don't know when my office door is closed whether I am counseling someone, working at my desk or on the sofa asleep. I have learned to do what I have to do then I can do what I want to do. Don't be so tough on yourself. Give yourself a break.

Don't be like the mother who said, "Johnny, bring home all A's." So Johnny brought home all A's and he came bursting through the door. He said, "Mommy, Mommy, I have all A's." She said, "Wipe your feet, wash your face, get ready for supper, go feed the dog." The poor kid; Mommy needs to learn to celebrate. Stop a moment, think about the things you did get done. Be good to yourself.

You live one life. In everything you do, you make a life. Everything you say, you create your circumstances. You will be victimized *more by yourself than you will be anybody else.* Life consists not in the abundance of things that you possess or what you will wear or what you will eat. There's more to life than that. Everything you do and everything you say, every response you give, every prayer you pray, every song you sing, every hand you shake, every smile you communicate, you are learning to build a life.

I heard about a man who was a carpenter. He worked for thirty years for a construction company. He walked into the boss's office one day and said, "You know that I will be retiring in sixty days."

"Yes, I realize that." The boss was never one to give anybody credit for anything, he just paid them their salary and sent them on their way. He never said a word of praise to anyone for anything. So he said to the man, "I do realize that you have sixty days left and I want you to build one last house before you leave. I want you to build it for me."

The man walked out of the office with a chip on his shoulder the size of a railroad tie. He was so mad. He said, "I have sixty days to fix him good and I am going to do it right." He set out to build the house. He built the house backwards, he did everything wrong just to be spiteful. If you put a marble in the middle of the floor it would roll either one direction or the other, if you flipped the light the doorbell rang, if you turned the water on in the kitchen it came on in the bathtub. Everything was a boobytrap. The guy felt real good about himself. He walked in and handed the keys to the boss and he said, "Here are the keys, the house is finished."

The boss stood up from behind the desk and he said, "Sir, you have worked faithfully for this company for thirty years and since you are retiring I would like to give you this house." He handed the keys back to him. You see he had to go and live in the mess that he had made. It took him years to dig under the flooring and in the ceilings and rewire and replumb everything.

Everyday you live, my friend, you are building the life that you live in. We get uptight about some of the most simple things. We have a way of getting our priorities really messed up. If we can all come to realization and awareness of personal worth and image, more importantly who He is and what He is to us and learn that life is temporal. Life is like the grass, it comes up in the morning and then it wears away. If everything that you put your hand to has to do with this life only, that means that this is where all of your treasures are. And that means that when you die, who will these things be?

If you put your heart first of all into Him—for where a man's treasure is there will his heart be also. Life consists not in the abundance of things one possesses. Life is more than meat, what you will eat, what you will wear. Somehow if we could rearrange all of this and take two steps forward to the foot of the cross, put your life in His hands and His hands in your hands and get a new perspective, a new grip on things. Put the 3 D's into action—Desire, Direction, Determination. You will feel the difference in your heart and life today.

Chapter 5

Thinking

I am constantly challenged by the knowledge that we have not yet brought this church to its fullest potential. That bothers me. You don't know how that bothers me. I ponder on it daily. It churns like a storm in my soul, twenty-four hours a day. And I am constantly reaching and searching for a way to somehow bring to fruition the many capabilities and the potential that is lying dormant, latent, if you will, in the souls and the bodies and the minds of God's great church.

However, in my search for answers to help you, as well as myself, to realize our full potential in the work of God, I am drawn to the Scripture written in Proverbs 23:7, and I think that it is what one might call a truism.

"For as he thinketh in his heart, so is he."

After much observation, after talking with thousands of individuals over a period of thirty plus years in the ministry, I have come to the conclusion that this Scripture, is true, in every sense of the word.

As one thinketh in his heart, so is he. No generation that has ever lived in the history of the world has been as blessed as this generation. Never before has such keen perception, brilliant reasoning and deductible fact been available to anyone who seeks it. We have inherited by virtue several reasons a tremendous opportunity. Not only as Bible college students, not only as potential pastors, evangelists, school principals, school teachers, music directors, but as good saints and soul winners in a local church we have inherited from several areas a tremendous set of circumstances which has set the stage and has removed from us certain hindrances and provided for us one of the most fabulous opportunities to make a mark in this world for God that any generation has ever known. Many of the things that were problems years ago, are not problems today. Many of the hurdles that the "old-timers" had to get over are not present today.

We have inherited a tremendous opportunity. The giants in every field of human endeavor have bequeathed their knowledge to us. We live in an age of ever present past, and we have inherited permanent truths that are forever important and do not diminish with age. Upon them you can build, you can live, and in them you can safely invest yourself. That can't be said about everything with which you get involved in this life. But when it comes to this truth, you can build on it; you can sink your teeth into it; it will stick to your ribs; it will give you strength; it is solid. And though all the rest of the world is on sinking sand, you can sing, "On Christ the Solid Rock I Stand."

If you have ever longed for something solid to stand on; if you have ever reached for something of a permanent nature, something that is not transitional, something that is not faddish, something that does not just come and go with the ebb and flow of time and tide, I'd like to tell you that this truth is that something. Oh, how wonderful it is to know you have found the truth.

I sat in a place of business yesterday afternoon in the city of Philadelphia, on Chestnut Street. There was something about the young man who appeared to be approximately thirty years of age that I was drawn to.

So I smiled often, kind of relaxed and made it a point to jest about whatever I could whenever I could. At the conclusion of the transaction, he leaned forward so that his associates standing near could not hear him discuss religion on the job. He said to me, "Mrs. Trout, it has been a pleasure to work with you."

And I leaned forward and I said, also in a hushed tone, "The pleasure was all mine." I had told him who I was. I had told him where I was from. I had told him what I do with my life. I had told him what I believe.

"I am a Hebrew," he said. I had suspicioned that, in that his name was Harvey Katz. Then he added, "But I am a Christian Hebrew."

"That's the only kind of Hebrew to be now a days," I answered.

He said, "It is so wonderful to have found the truth." And when he said "truth," I could feel it rise out of his soul.

"But Harvey, let me tell you something," I replied.

"What?"

We were whispering; and the associates were standing ten feet away watching us.

"You know most traditional Christians believe in a trinity of gods. When you came from the Hebrew faith of one God, did you accept that from them?" I asked.

"Well they told me that I would never be able to understand it, that I would just have to accept it by faith," he answered.

"Harvey, I have good news for you, you don't have to accept it by faith, you don't even have to accept it!"

"What do you mean by that?"

"There are not three persons in a trinity of Gods. That's paganistic, that came out of Rome," I continued.

He stopped, looked down and said, "You know you're right."

"I know I'm right. The Jehovah you worshipped in the Old Testament is the Jesus you serve now," I added.

He grinned from ear to ear and said, "You know that makes it a whole lot easier for me to accept Jesus as the Messiah. And I believe that Jesus is the Messiah."

And then I said to him, "Harvey, have you ever read the Book of the Acts of the Apostles?"

And he looked away; he was a little embarrassed that he did not know what I was talking about.

"You know in the New Testament there's Matthew, Mark, Luke, John then the Book that's called the Acts of the Apostles," I said.

"Oh, yeah."

"Have you ever read it?" I queried.

"Well I can't say that I have," he replied hesitantly.

"Man, if you think this is great, go home and read it."

"I'll do it," he decided.

"And pay special attention to the second chapter, and notice what happened on the Feast Day of Pentecost," I said carefully.

"I'll do it tonight."

"Would you call me and let me know what happens?"

"Yes I will, I'll be in touch," he promised.

I can't wait to get his phone call. Hallelujah!

He said, "The truth of all of this is tremendous!" And when he would say *truth,* something would just rumble in his voice. And he is so excited that he knows the truth and he knows that Jesus is the Messiah and now he knows that He is Jehovah.

Truth you can build your own stairway to heaven on. You can come from anything to this, but you can't go from this to anything. And so after Chapter Four's dissertation on "Life," you're asking, "Now what do I do?"

Brother Trout came home Monday night, and with his hands on his hips he said to me, "The next time you preach on the 3 D's you should plan to stay in the office all day Monday explaining to people how they can do it." He said, "I've had at least a dozen conferences today as a result of your sermon." He said, "If you're gonna preach it, you stand by to help counsel it."

"The 3 D's? Do you know what the 3 D's are?" I asked.

"Yes, I know what they are: Desire, Direction, Determination; I heard it all day long," he added.

But sometimes, I am guilty of stirring people up and then not giving them direction. I would like to follow up Chapter Four on "Life" with some instruction that will be helpful to give you direction so you won't be shooting horses, thinking they are deer! Now, I, in all fairness to Sister Tammy, must tell you the meaning of the word *hypothetical.* Some of you didn't catch that. No she didn't shoot a horse. That was just all—or did she?

If you are going to have direction in what you are doing, if you are going to get anywhere and get anything done, there are some basic truths and principals that you must build on. I am constantly amazed at how little direction many people have. I have often said that we, as a group, do so well, when we do so many things accidentally and haphazardly. I wonder what could happen if we ever held committee meetings and planned them. You talk about turning this world upside down! And so I come down to some very important facts, principles and concepts I would like to share with you.

The Scripture provides the basic setting for this entire chapter and it's about, "Thinking." For several thousand years, from the ancient Egyptian tidal measurements of the Nile to the present day telemetering of the controls in the modern satellite program, the advance of science has been so spectacular we have marveled at the wonder of man's scientific progress. Yet the greatest intellectual advance of all time has been within the people themselves. Not necessarily what they have invented but the inventions have become an off-shoot or a result of the improvement of the intelligence within the men that invented them.

Sometimes we look at the invention and we ignore the fact that a man thought it up. But that same kind of improvement in the intelligence of man is present within your own mind and being. It is a mistake for God's people to become so heavenly minded that they're no earthly good. And when all our spiritual experience revolves around only prayer and only Bible reading and it has no fruit, no product, no benefit anywhere else, then I think we need to back up and take another look lest we grow inwardly, and as stars that fall inward, we destroy ourselves.

The praying is necessary. The Bible reading is necessary. What happens at the altar is necessary. But it cannot stop there. I could motivate you to do things, but if your motivation is simply instructional or inspiration, then you go out and it dies before you get past the first paragraph. But if what you concede to the hands of God, if what you consecrate to Him here, if what you dedicate to Him here, becomes a goal, and an objective and a purpose, and you go out and do the things you promised God you're going to do, then you'll begin to see results. Then you're going to become a faithful Christian. Then you will begin to say, "I have been something for God."

To say, "I love God" is not enough. A man that tells his wife he loves her and then ignores her all of the time is a foolish man. A woman that says to her husband, "I love you darling," but then ignores him the other 23 3/4 hours of the day is just talking. So to come to church and say, "I love you God," to pray and say, "I love you God, and I want to serve God and I want to do something for God," and then to walk out and do absolutely nothing, after a point this becomes a set of mocking circumstances. We make fools of ourselves. We become hypocrites, and this concerns me. If this church could ever put wheels, legs, arms, mouth, ears, eyes and nose on everything we say, what could we do for God?

You carry within you the seeds of potential, and even greatness. But you will never obtain any lofty goal until you give birth to it. You carry within you, just as every woman who is biologically normal has within her, the potential to bear children. We never see its face, nor hear its cry until she goes through a certain set of circumstances and that also includes patience and labor, weeping and pain. But eventually she gives birth to that child and then that which was nothing more than a gleam in its father's eye is visible and audible.

So are many of our consecrations. We say things. We desire noble dreams, we dream. But we must learn to continue beyond that, carry that dream, carry that desire, carry that burden, implement it, give birth to it through agony, through pain, through prayer, through fasting, through working, through doing. Putting our mouth and/or feet and/or person where our words are. Giving body and action to the things that we have only said. Then we will begin to realize, and taste the fruit of our labor. Thus, through human thoughts, thoughts that are in alignment with the Word of God, you can design a plan of victory for your life. Let this mind be in you that was in Christ. Every day He lived, every step He took, every word He spoke, every action He made, the wave of every hand movement, the direction of His eyes, the path that He walked upon, everything had a purpose and a direction.

He did not go to Calvary the day He was born in Bethlehem, but in His own mind and heart He knew that's where He was headed. He did not go to Calvary the day He stood in the Temple, but somehow He knew. He stood and talked with the disciples and He admonished them that He would not always be with them. He made statements like, "For this cause came I into the world." Purpose, direction, positive, certain; all of these things were effects of His nature and His activity. The essential truth of the Scripture in Proverbs 23:7, "As a man thinketh in his heart, so is he," not only embraces the whole of a man's being, but it is so comprehensive as to reach out to every condition and circumstance of his life, "As a man thinketh in his heart, so is he."

Now I could spend one hour right there, but let me stop for a moment to give you illustrations to be sure you are following me. A person that thinks jealous thoughts in his heart is always defensive of his position. A person who steals, suspects others to be thieves. An individual who will lie is always reluctant to believe someone else, even though they may be telling the truth. "As a man thinketh in *his* heart, so is he." His thinking is an expose of what he is. If he is unfaithful to his companion, he suspects everyone else. And so it is not only a matter of the heart that is in jeopardy; it is a matter of the mind and the thought pattern that is jeopardized by wrong or bad thinking.

It is the atmosphere and the conditions around that individual that are affected by the way he thinks. The atmosphere in the home is set by the way the parent thinks. The way children are, is a direct result of how the parents have thought. In most instances, children mirror parents. They are reflections of the atmosphere in which they have grown. We find that hard to accept when things go sour. Nevertheless, if we are honest with ourselves in the privacy of our minds, we can dig around in the closed and locked closets and find enough garbage to substantiate the truism, and the fact remains. A person is literally what he thinks—his character being the complete sum of all his thoughts.

You (and this may surprise you) are the master of your thoughts. Don't blame it on God and don't blame it on the devil. You, sweetheart, you! You are the master of your thoughts. This is one arena where you rule supremely. This is one stage where you are the sole actor. This is the one speech where you are the single voice. Nobody, including the devil, can dictate your thoughts. Your mind is your personal private domain. It is your kingdom. You alone rule upon its throne. You make the laws. You rescind them. You are the police that monitors the entrance or the exit of thoughts. You and you alone are to be blamed for what you think. Until you reach a place in your self-discipline where you are willing to throw the yoke upon your mind, put the harness on, put the bit in its mouth and yank the reins good, it will continue to run rampant and serve destruction to everything it comes near.

Your thoughts, your mind, is a chamber which *no one* can enter without your permission, including the devil. If you accept thoughts that are negative, that are "anti"-Philippians 2, if they come in there it's because you permitted their entrance. And most of the time they enter because you are standing at the door watching for something to substantiate another thought that should not have been let in to begin with. And he's back there lurking in the corner, waiting for documentation and substantiation. His name is *Suspicion.* I propose that 99.9% of the depression, mental agony, discouragement, your throw-in-the-towel syndrome, your sick-and-tired-of-it-all situation, would come to an abrupt halt if you would put a screeching brake on the mind pattern. Throw up the guard at the door. Throw everything out that's not right. Clean house, I mean clean house, and start all over.

You ask, "How do you clean house, Sister Trout?" I'll tell you when I clean, I clean on my knees. That's how I clean my mind. You just have to do it every now and then. You know things creep in and they hide in the corners. And see, I had to open the door and let them in. I left the door open, and I should not have left it unguarded. Nevertheless, they got in there. After a bit I see an accumulation and the accumulation draws my attention because I notice that I am reacting in certain ways. And I'm starting to wonder, "Why am I like this?" And then I'll stop and I'll look around and I'll say, "Well, how did you get in here?" Then I'll realize that I have permitted the entrance of certain thoughts into my mind that are negative, unsubstantiated and sometimes evil. So I have to go clean house, clean house on my knees. Pray, pray, pray, PRAY, pray, pray.

And when I get wreckless on my knees, honey, every devil in hell better take to his heels and get going. When I get enough of that stuff and I get tired of getting drug all over the creation, I take so much of it and then I clean house. I get tired of feeling down and out and drug out and depressed and discouraged and when I sit up and take notice and say, "What in the world is going on here?," I beat it for the other end of the house and close the door and wage war. I guarantee when I start waging war on my knees I go through every room and I scrub the walls down. I take the closet doors off the hinges. I yank and pull and I throw out. And then I let the Holy Ghost come in like a cool breeze and it blows all that stuff away and then I set the fire to it and let the Holy Ghost fire burn it out. When God and I get through with my mind, she's as fresh as a daisy. Hallelujah!

Your mind may be likened to a garden which may be intelligently cultivated or allowed to run wild. But whether neglected or cultivated, it must and it will bring forth. There is neutral circumstance here. If no useful seeds are put into it, then an abundance of useless weeds will come up and continue to produce after their kind. So you are going to have to be careful what kind of seeds are dropped into the garden of your mind.

Now let me give you a little word of warning—watch out for the birds, they'll get you in trouble. Someone says, "How did you find that out?" A little bird told me.

Let me tell you about a little bird that could have gotten me in trouble. Our good friend is Jerry Pepper who is with the State Police, one of the top men on the force. As a state policeman, that's one area of his life, but another is he raises Arabian horses, so he and Brother Trout talk very often. One spring day he was out at our house, we were standing out at the front of the sidewalk at the carport area. Brother Trout and Jerry and I were just standing there talking. It was a nice day and I looked over and there was this very tall, ugly weed, that was in the beautiful boxwoods. We had been so busy we hadn't pulled weeds and done all those things you have to do to keep a yard looking nice, we just kind of snatched and grabbed on the run. But as we were talking, I walked over there and I thought I didn't want to make it too obvious that I had this ugly weed in my garden so I just took the toe of my shoe and tipped it over on the ground and broke it where it came up out of the ground, and thought "I'll pick it up later" and went on talking. Then after a bit I thought "What's the difference," and I reached over and picked it up and started across the driveway to throw it out towards the woods.

"You know what that is don't you?" Jerry called.

"A weed." I didn't know what kind it was.

"It's marijuana," he said.

I said, "Wouldn't *State News* love that?"

STATE POLICEMAN FINDS MARIJUANA GROWING IN THE PREACHER'S YARD

We had a big laugh and I said, "You have got to be kidding!" Of course Jerry thought it was really funny because he could see I was embarrassed that marijuana had grown this high in my front yard.

And I said, "Well to be honest with you, that's the first

time I had ever seen any."

He held it in his hand and then he began to explain it to me. He said, "See this saw tooth blade type of leaf on it and see that there are three sections." It was marijuana. It was—no doubt, it was.

And I said, "But how did it get here?"

And he said, "A bird dropped the seed right there. It happens often," he said. "Notice when you're passing a soy bean field you may wonder why you see one or two or three lone stalks of corn growing in the middle of a soy bean field. It's because of the birds flying with the seeds in their mouth and drop the seed and so where they're dropped, they grow."

I surely was glad he understood. But it certainly proves a point, and it gave me a tremendous lesson about my mind. So watch the little birdie that tells you things. Do not let people dump their garbage into your mind. Just as a garden must be cultivated to bring forth good things, so may a person cultivate his mind, weeding out all the wrong. Unless you do this you are going to be in trouble. You need to weed out the useless, unpure, unkind thoughts that go in.

You command the soul of your being out of which your circumstances grow. The soul attracts that which it secretly harbors. "As the man thinketh in his heart, so is he." The soul attracts that. Light begets light. Each after its own kind. And so if you harbor in your mind things that do not belong there, they will attract, like a magnet, those kind of things, that which it loves and that which it fears. It either reaches the height of its cherished ambition or it falls to the level of circumstance. Circumstance does not *make* a man. It simply *reveals* him. Circumstance will bring out what is really in you. You do not become certain things on certain days. You are what you are twenty-four hours a day and the circumstances which surround you simply illuminate your weaknesses or your strengths.

I have seen women put in the most extenuating set of circumstances and I have seen as a result of that pressure such tremendous character, a noble mind that became apparent and evident to all of us. Place another woman, who thinks differently in her heart, in the same set of circumstances and you will see opposing results.

You cannot blame your circumstances for what you are. You are what you are. The circumstances will either bring it out, illuminate it, strengthen it or put pressure on it to improve. Be careful, and never be ruled by your circumstances. Learn to take charge of your life. Get on top of things, don't cower down under them. We give in and give up too quickly—far too quickly. In most circumstances that are very distasteful, unattractive to us, the first tendency is to shrink, back away, bow out. Let those circumstances strengthen your position. Your character is revealed by circumstances.

Men do not attract that which they *want.* They attract that which they *are.* You are bound only by yourself. Why don't you set yourself free and let yourself be. It's fun to fly up above it all. Rise above it. Rise above it.

When it gets real heavy for me, I spread my wings and fly, way up there. And I found that if I view things from that perspective then I can find them more tolerable.

Thoughts and actions are the jailers of faith. They either imprison or they liberate you. So you've got to get serious with yourself. You've got to zero in on yourself and your actions. Those two elements in your life hold the key. They will either imprison you or they will unlock the door and let you go. The choice is yours.

Many are anxious to improve their circumstances but are unwilling to improve themselves. When you improve yourself, you will have automatically improved your circumstances. Good thoughts and actions do not produce bad results.

Did not James talk about that in his letter? He said, "Can an olive tree bear figs or a fig tree bear olive berries? Does a fountain send forth both bitter and sweet water?" No. It's a fact you can't escape. So if you have good thoughts and you have good actions, you'll get good results. If you have bad thoughts and bad actions, you are going to get bad results. That's a scriptural premise.

There are so many things going for us. So many things happening that we can become involved in. The work of God has never been more exciting than it is today. There have never been more opportunities to be involved in the work of God, actively and personally, as there are today. It's tremendous and yet in God's great church there are three kinds of people. There's that first group of people who make things happen; and then secondly, there's a group of people who watch things happen; and thirdly, there are those who go around asking, "What happened?" We need the desire to charge ahead, not to just be charged and expect to run like a battery until we run down. But to get the action within us and go through and put into action all of the desires that we have been harboring in our hearts for all of this time. Some people are so pessimistic about every thing.

The pessimist is a man who says, "What kind of day could it possibly be when you have to wake up in the morning to face it?" Some say I want to do great things but I can't get motivated. Have you ever heard that? Well, you'll learn to deal with motivation as a principal.

Now the word *motivation* is not a bad word. Motivation is a principal that we must learn to live with and work with. Some do not even want to consider motivation. They only say, "Give me facts." How can I get the job done, without having constantly to drive and be motivated or motivate others. We have had preachers and pastors come in here and they watch the way this thing runs and the way the people work and the way everything goes together. Then they come to us and they ask, "How do you get all of these people to do all of this?" And I'm standing there trying to figure out how it all comes together and I kind of know, but I kind of don't know either. It's a combination of several things. And I don't really know how to describe it. It's very frustrating to some pastors to come into a situation like this and watch a church operate like the people in this church operate within this work. It's frustrating to them, rather than encouraging because they don't know where to start. And I've had them say to me, "Do you have to constantly keep pumping the people just to keep them motivated?" Then I have had people say to me, "Well I just can't handle that. I'm not going to give in and get going on this motivational thing and if you have to motivate people all the time then just forget it." Those kind of people never do anything. They had twenty in church ten years ago, they had twenty in church five years and they had twenty in church last Sunday and they will have eighteen next Sunday. If that's the way they want to live and do their work, well that's their problem and not mine. God bless them! I couldn't live that way, quite honestly. There's too much to do to sit around and get aggravated at someone else who's doing it.

Some people don't even like to consider motivation as a fact. Because, number one, in order to motivate somebody else, you have to be motivated yourself and that could possibly be where the problem lies. Now that's a dilemma! It really is. No matter which way you go with that one you lose. It's like a deep sea diver that got a message on his radio, while he was way down there, he heard the captain say, "Come up quick, the ship is sinking."

They say, "Just give me facts. Stay away from the emotional things. No motivation, no hard hitting drives." I have heard people criticize Anthony Mangun for the hard-hitting, fast-moving pace that they take in their church. But the same people that criticize them are also running twenty. You know there are some people that are deaf, some that are dumb, and some that are blind, and occasionally you run up on one that is deaf, dumb *and* blind. You have to be way off track to be running twenty for ten years and criticize somebody who has built a church to 1,500 people.

They say principles don't count, but theories and ideas are foundations and principles that are written in the Bible. There are theories and ideas that must be converted into some kind of results. So you take the theory and the ideas, then you apply the Energy Principle. The Energy Principle is what I am calling, "Motivation." If you don't like the word *motivation* then say *Energy Principle.* It's all the same thing. The theory or the idea is, "Johnny, clean up your room." The Energy Principle is, "Or I'm gonna give you a spanking." That's the motivation!

There are three different ways to motivate or three different ways motivation works as an energy source. (1) It helps us to do the things that we did not do before. A ship is safe in a harbor, granted, it doesn't have to worry about the high seas, doesn't need a navigator. Most or many people are content to rest in the harbor of God's love. No storms on the high seas. But I want you to also take note to that ship. It will never deliver the goods to another harbor. It will never pick up a passenger and transfer it to another part of the world.

If you want to dock your little ship in this harbor and stay safe from storm, sweetheart, you are just as welcome as the flowers in May. I love you and you can stay right here in this little warm cozy place and just let us hug you and pat you on the back and encourage you and lift you up and help carry you along when you get down. If that's the thing you want, you are in the greatest place in the world. This is a harbor. It's warm! It's safe! It's pretty! It's nice! It's enjoyable—all of those things.

But you're looking at one lady who wants to get the ship out of the harbor on to the high seas. I want to deliver the goods. I want to pick up the passengers. I want to bring some back. I want some movement. I want some action. I want some results.

A person who prefers not to be motivated never makes any waves and he never accomplishes anything. The person who is willing to take a risk (not a chance there's a difference, you take a chance when you play the lottery, you take a risk when you launch out to do something for God) is going to go places. (2) The ability to be. Unique personality—that which everyone of you has. Different—everyone individually in your own right. Your success is determined by the way your individual personality is developed in relationship to your talent.

The Scripture teaches us that it is not wise to compare

yourselves among yourselves. So do not try to mark up to my standards nor keep my pace. Forget that, you probably would not live a week! But if that's what I want to do, just let me go. Don't get in my way. But don't think you have to do it like I do it. Remember that you have the ability to be, in relationship to talents God gave you. God gave you an individual personality. He gave you individual talents and you are only in competition with God's requirements of what He gave to you.

We do not want a stereotype church. This is not a "cookie cutter" institution. All I am asking for you to do is look around and see what God put in you and get after it. You can do some things I cannot do. You can talk to people I will never reach. You will touch people I will never meet. When we get this thing together, dear friends, it's going to send earth tremors around the world. Some people are motivated to climb mountains. I personally have no desire to climb a mountain. Some people are motivated to write books. Some people are motivated to start works or build churches. Others are motivated to sit around and do nothing but criticize those who do. So you see there is talent in all of us!

Motivation, it is that source of energy that gets us off dead center. Let me reiterate. It is not what you have that counts, it's what you do with what you have that counts. If every one of you that can teach home Bible studies would teach home Bible studies the church would be quadrupled by Sunday. The most talented person in the world accomplishes nothing unless he puts his talents to work—putting energy principles to work. Motivation. Achievement. Motivation. There are a lot of books on it and I have done a lot of reading on it. If there is any one thing I have lots of books about it is management and motivation. I am still trying to learn everything I can get my hands on. I study lots of books, lots of methods of achievement motivation relative to the business world and corporate management, etc. But the one thing that I have gleaned from all this reading and that I can relate very well to is this concept.

When you set up goals, don't look at the past. Look at the future. If any one of us looked at the past we would not do anything. It is too discouraging. So when you set your goals, don't set your goals in relationship to what you did—or did not do—yesterday. It could have been a bad scene. Close the door on yesterday. It's done, it's gone, it's said, you cannot retract it, you cannot change it. If you go back and try to fix it you cannot mend it. So forget it. And start now. Look at the future. Then set yourself a time table and set some standards and then get after it! Remember every saint has a past, but every sinner has a future. We know we do not have to depend on what we were or what it was like in order to achieve our goals. This is the marvelous thing about all of this. What you were yesterday has absolutely nothing to do with your potential for tomorrow.

There is no other circumstance in the world that can afford that liberty. When you walk into any business or institution to seek employment, the first thing they are going to ask you for is a resume and secondly they want to know what was the last job and why did you quit. So your past follows you in the business world.

But when it comes to doing business in the Kingdom of God, when it comes to working and being fruitful in this situation here, you know what? You can bar and lock the door to yesterday. You do not have to make reference to what you were. Nobody is permitted to go back there and drag anything up and say you can't do this because you were that. Oh, no! The Apostle said, after giving that list of awful things, "Such were some of you, but you are washed, you are clean." Hallelujah! This is a new day. This is Genesis. This is the beginning. You can start all over.

So you failed. So you made a mistake. So you threw in the towel. So you gave up. That was yesterday. Don't make any plans based on yesterday. Look at the here and now. Get a hold of this thing and let's get after it and do something for God.

We can be different tomorrow from what we were today because we had today to practice. Nothing can be more important to you in all of this than self-confidence. That is a measure, your measure of your ability to perform a task. When we believe we can accomplish something, we see good results. Then we will have the confidence to do it again the next time.

All of the circumstances that come together to make things happen did so because someone put them together. Nothing in the natural life automatically happens. Somebody did it. Somebody dug the hole. Somebody mixed the mortar. Somebody laid the block. Somebody did everything you see in this place. There is a network of activity that makes Kent Christian Center a phenomenal center in which to do something for God and it does not just happen. There are dozens of people that are doing what is being done. None of it is accidental. Somebody turns the lights on. Somebody turns them off. Somebody turns the thermostat on. Nothing is automatic. People doing things. How much are you involved in what is going on in the work of God? The Apostle Paul said it, "I can do all things through

Christ who strengtheneth me." When you want to do something badly enough you figure out a way to do it.

I heard about the hippie selling watches on the streets of San Francisco. Somebody walked up and said, "How much are your watches?"

"Twenty dollars."

"What did you pay for them?" the man asked.

"Twenty dollars," the hippie replied.

"Wait a minute, you're selling the watches for twenty dollars, you're paying twenty dollars. You're not making any money man, where's the profit?" the man quizzed.

"Repairs, man, repairs," the hippie answered.

When you really want to do something badly enough, you will figure out how to do it. Deliberately plan. As a man thinketh in his heart, what is the rest of it?—so is he. All your moods are created by your mind. When you feel depressed, it is because you are dominated by negative thoughts. Who let them in? You want to get rid of your depression? Open the door and kick them out. The conclusion is, in most instances, our negative thoughts are false and are based on false principles.

Thoughts of positive faith will displace negative thoughts of fear that have been holding you back. If the church does not grow, it is not because the losers or the lazies did not do anything. It is because the doers did not.

In conclusion, let us consider your mind. When Satan wanted to leave his evil influence upon the human race, he led the first man and woman into sin and the first thing he did was attack the woman's mind. II Corinthians 11:3 says (ASV):

> *"But I am afraid less as a serpent deceived Eve*

by his craftiness your minds should be led astray from the simplicity and purity of devotion to Christ."

Why would the devil want to attack your mind? Because your mind is the part of the image of God where God communicates with you and reveals His will to you. You are made in the image of God and in His likeness He created you. And it is in your mind that God communicates with you. So when Satan wants to prohibit this activity, he doesn't give you a black eye. He does not step on your toe. He does not kick you in the shin, punch you in the stomach or hit you across the head. He very simply, quietly and subtly attacks your mind because that is where you communicate with God. If he can somehow abort or break this line of communication he won't have to give you a black eye, punch you in the stomach, hit you over the head or kick you in the shins. You'll do all of that to yourself—all by yourself.

It is unfortunate that some people have minimized the significance of the mind because the Bible does emphasize its importance. Paul wrote to the Colossians in 3:9, 10.

"Do not lie to one another since you have laid aside the old self with its evil practices and have put on the new self who is being renewed to a true knowledge according to the one who created him."

"This I say therefore and affirm together with the Lord that you walk no longer just as the Gentiles walked in the futility of their mind being darkened in their understanding excluded from the life of God because of the ignorance that is in them, because of the hardness of their heart and they hav-

ing become calloused have given themselves over to sensuality for the practice of every kind of impurity with greediness. But you did not learn Christ in this way, if indeed you have heard Him and have been taught in Him just as truth is in Jesus that in reference to your former manner of life you lay aside the old self which is being corrupted in accordance with the lust of deceit and that you be renewed in the spirit of your mind and put on the new self which in the likeness of God has been created in righteousness and holiness of truth" (Ephesians 4:17-24).

Then Paul wrote to the Romans and said,

"And be not conformed to this world: but be ye transformed by the renewing of your mind, that ye may prove what is that good, and acceptable, and perfect will of God" (Romans 12:2).

So God renews our mind. He renews our minds through His truth, this truth of the Word of God. In John 17:17, Jesus is praying:

"Sanctify them in the truth, thy word is truth."

So if Satan can get you to believe a lie then he will work in your life to lead you into sin. And the mind is where it all starts. This is why Satan attacks your mind. You must protect your mind from the attacks of the wicked one.

"Finally brethren whatever is true, whatever is honorable, whatever is right, whatever is pure,

whatever is lovely, whatever is of good repute, if there is any excellence and anything is worthy of praise, let your mind dwell on these things'' (Philippians 4:8).

Paul is saying, if it is not true don't let it in! In recent years science has discovered many fascinating things about the human mind. It is like a computer. Your mind can store facts, and impressions and even emotions and recall them years later. Your mind can reach into the past through your memory. It can reach into the future through your imagination. Your thinking affects your feeling and your will. ''For as he thinks within himself, so is he.'' The doctor says you are what you eat. The Bible says you are what you think. And the devil knows the tremendous power of the mind and that is why he tries to capture it for himself.

Isaiah says:

''The steadfast of mind thou wilt keep in perfect peace because he trusts in thee'' (Isaiah 26:3).

Paul says:

''For the mind set on the flesh is death but the mind set on the spirit is life and peace'' (Romans 8:6).

So your mind affects your whole being. While I do not totally agree with the success psychology and the so-called healing psychology of our day, I must admit that attitudes are important to your physical health and success in life. The exciting new field of holistic medicine draws upon the influences of the mind to help the patient cure himself, but that borderlines some questions and holistic medicine right now is way out yonder on the wait-and-see-shelf for me. It smacks too much of Sigmund Freud.

And so as he thinks in his heart, so he is.

If you can close your mind, close your eyes right now and think in your heart. Look around. You should get a fairly accurate appraisal of what you are and when you finish that, say, as the Apostle Paul said, "I can do all things through Christ who strengtheneth me."

My prayer is that God will give us a breath of the Holy Spirit that will sweep across us and that every person reading this book will lay it down with a renewed mind. If you read the Bible at all, you should have a vague idea of the kinds of things that are permitted in your mind and the kinds of things that are prohibited. I don't think you need another sermon. I don't think you'll need to ring my phone or call my office and ask Sister Trout, "Is this wrong, Is this wrong?" Really and truly some of these things you have to learn to answer for yourself.

You can open your eyes. Let the Holy Ghost come in right now and like a cool breeze just blow across the rooms of your mind. I would like for you to search. I want you to go into the sealed chambers where no one, including God, has been permitted to enter. I want you to get the lock, turn the combination, take it off, open the door and let it go free. Grievances, unforgiving spirit, jealousy, hatred, envying, strife, vainglory, pride, stubbornness, anger, sensuality, licentiousness, lying, stealing, conniving, deceiving—the list goes on; it's endless. It is 6,000 years old. How could I name it all now. Whatever is in there, that does not belong, I want to unlock the door and let it out and let it go free. You don't have to tell anybody anything. You don't need to confess anything to me. You don't need to go around confessing to other people. Really and truly you are probably the only one you will have to forgive, because you have been so mad with yourself about these things for so long, until you are the only one it concerns. As soon as you can forgive yourself, close the door on yesterday and walk into tomorrow with face lifted into the rising sun. Spread your wings and fly away, like a bird—free from any encumbrances; free from the bondage. You say yet not free from the problem? That's true, that is right. The problem may still be there but you are different. Problems are still there to be dissolved but *you are different.*

God is moving in this world today. I feel the Spirit in a ministry of helps. Can you feel the Holy Ghost moving in your heart? In the name of Jesus, cast out every doubt and fear and intimidation and hatred and bitterness and envy and strife and vainglory and perverseness and waywardness and thievery and lying and stealing, any thoughts that are negative, that are downcast, that are depressing in the name of Jesus. He will let you go free! Ask God to let the mind of Christ be in you. Then spread your wings and fly! You can rise to heights you have never known. Let the peace that passeth all understanding rule in your heart.

Oh Holy Ghost, renew our minds, that we may speak clearly and positively and be certainly motivated to charge into the work of God which You've called us to do. I pray, Oh Lord, that You will liberate Your church. Set us free, Lord. Let Your people go forth with such fervor like a marching army charging against the gates of hell. Let its results resound around the world. In the name of Jesus.

I pray for healing of old wounds, Lord. Scars from the past that haunt people from day to day. I charge the enemy of the soul that he is never to approach the door of the mind again. I forbid him entrance. Oh God, give every man, woman, boy and girl a new slate to write the events of his history upon. Slip into the hand of every man and woman who reads this chapter a pen to make the plan to set the direction, to set the goals, and live the standards, by which each of them shall begin anew; a great work in the kingdom of God. From the students to the saints, from the teachers to the preachers, from the musicians to the ushers, from the front to the back, from the side to the side, from depth to the circumference of this place let it resound with the energy of God. Let the Holy Ghost propel us out of our laziness, out of our lethargy and into the freeway. Let us charge into the territory of the enemy and burst asunder the things that bind and through the power of the Holy Ghost set men free. Liberty, liberty, liberty. Wings to fly. Wheels to roll. Power to go. Strength to work. Of this we pray in Jesus' name, amen.

Remember nobody ever reached the goal from a sitting position. Nobody ever won a race sitting in the grand stand. Nobody ever carried the football past the goal post sitting on the side lines. Nobody. It's the people who *run* that *win* games. It's people who *work* that *get jobs done.* It's people who *pray* and *have faith* that *move mountains.* It's people that do what they know how to do. Nobody ever reached a goal from a chair. No job was ever accomplished just talking about it. He has given you the individuality to be, the ability to become. Reach, reach, stretch, stand, walk, run, practice, drive, go, move, do it. Do it tonight. Do it again in the morning. Do it tomorrow afternoon. Do it tomorrow night. Do it next week. Get after it.

Where are you going? What are you doing? Where are you? What is on your mind? For where a man's treasure is, there will his heart be also. I cannot even begin to fathom the mighty work of the Holy Ghost that is going on in the world right now. There are people who are reaching into God and reaching a dimension in the Spirit that you have cried for, longed for, reached for, desired for; and you are going after it. And it's not going to die. It won't end when you close your eyes tonight. It's not going to come to a conclusion at the end of the week. I feel something happening that is going to live on next week and next month and next year and until Jesus comes. And the world is going to hear from you.

You'll never be the same. When God gets through with you and you get through with God, you'll never be the same. I pray when you have finished this book, you will not think the same. You won't be the same. You'll not walk the same. You'll not talk the same. Everything is going to have a different flavor. Everything is going to have a different atmosphere. Everything will have a new outlook. It's going to be different now. You will notice first of all that you are going to be *free*. You are going to be free from the thing that you just unlocked. You will no longer be laden by thoughts that you kept harbored. But you took the lock off and you opened the door, and the Holy Ghost flew through there and took them away. They are gone. You won't be bothered with them any more. They are gone. They don't exist. And even if you get weak and try to capture them, you won't be able to reach them because God has removed them so far from you.

There is a sleeping giant in this world today. God's church is a giant that has started to rouse itself. I feel it moving. There is a rumbling. There is a wind blowing. Glory! Hallelujah!

Come out from among them. Status quo. Same old thing. Just anybody. Just any saint. Normal. Oh no, no more. It's over. "Come out from among them and be ye separate," saith God. Do your thing for God. Whatever it is, do it! Do it! You can do it. You can do it well. Some of you are in training. God has called you to a place for training. I compliment you. I want to compliment you for taking the time. Thousands did not do it. But let me tell you something else. Those thousands that were not willing to take the time out of their life to do what you have done, you will overtake them and surge ahead of them before the story is told. Students in this Bible College set your heart, set your mind. Give it your best. Every pace, every lesson, every class, every note, every prayer meeting, every conflict, every encounter, every song, every moment of every day. Get after it. Drive, walk, run, go, sing, pray, preach, practice, witness, teach, move, move, move, move, MOVE!

The end of the race, and the goal to be reached is not as far away as you think it is. The curtain is liable to fall on this thing any minute. He could put His hands through the eastern sky and beckon us to come home. You may not even get the opportunity to do what you have resolved in His will to do. He may come. But won't it be great, going up when you are already flying? Won't it be great to go up when you are already soaring? Won't it be great to go up when you are already running?

What do you want to do now? The service is yours. It's all yours. I have mixed emotions. I would like to run laps around the building. I would like to find a corner and weep myself into the spirit of travail. I would like to pray with somebody else. I would like to pray by myself. I have mixed emotions. I don't know what I want to do. What do you want to do? Why don't you just do what you want to do right now?

Chapter 6

Coping With Depression

IN THE LAYMAN

Upon reading the twenty-third Psalm in my study of this subject, I had a very strong feeling that perhaps David was either in or on his way out of depression when he wrote this. We are going to describe depression and when we finish hopefully you will have a better understanding of exactly what it is and how it works.

The decade of anxiety by which the 70's were known has now given way to the melancholia of the 80's. We sense a national syndrome that is going through our country, but I look over a cross section of the United Pentecostal Church International spirit-filled people and I am picking up a syndrome that is going through many of our people. Those of us involved in God's work in a more intricate manner than others will have to recognize that we have not been exempt from this trend toward what is known as "depression." Perhaps there is no other involvement in human existence or vocation that is more frequently inclined toward depression than living for God because of the extreme highs and extreme lows that the human nature can experience during spiritual encounters. As far as the ministry is concerned, it has even been termed as an occupational hazard. When one gets very deeply involved in a ministry (whether in Christian Day School work, interpersonal relations with staff on a day to day basis, interaction with personnel within the church framework, or being a Christian rubbing elbows real often with other people—any position of leadership) there is what is called an occupational hazard—depression.

Depression will rob you if it is not understood and not coped with effectively. As a Christian, it will rob you of your witness and of your effectiveness. There have not been just a few, but many, who have been left in a debilitating condition as well as some who have ultimately lost out with God. As a matter of fact, as I mentally recall people who have backslidden, it seems to me that many of them failed during times of what we would term *a depression that was not adequately dealt with.*

Unfortunately many of us have bouts with depression and these times are antagonized, aggravated, or intensified by feelings of guilt and failure which stem from erroneous notions about the nature of depression. And because we do not understand it, we have a tendency to react to it in an adverse manner causing us to succumb to it and eventually be defeated by it. I think that when we finish this study you will have learned that depression is not a curse and it is not necessarily a bad thing.

Depression

The Word *depression* leaves you with a negative feeling, but I would like to help you change that so if you ultimately find yourself experiencing depression, you can, with some amount of ease, just kind of lean back, grin and say, "I'm okay. It will feel good when it quits hurting. It is all a part of what is supposed to happen." So—relax about the subject.

Some may be thoroughly mystified by the nature of their condition when they find themselves depressed, but there is hope I believe that much of this depression can be avoided altogether and that you can cope more effectively with depression that comes to you. I want to point out that often depression results from the nature of your walk with God. We term it, as in Paul's writings, as the war or the battle between flesh and the spirit. We do not know how to react to those battles and as a result have guilt, then fear. A little later on we will discuss this chain reaction. At the end of this series of events the ultimate has happened and you wonder how in the world you got there. What I am saying in a nutshell is, do not blame depression upon your weakness in every case. Sometimes situations come just due to the fact that your walk with God is ANTI—anti-body, anti-natural, anti-world. You are running the opposite direction on a street where everyone is going the other way! It isn't always that you are doing something wrong or that you have something to feel guilty about. Try to understand why you come to feel as you do in some situations.

The purposeful nature of depression is in providing a time to withdraw (which is so very important), to recoup, to put things into perspective. It will lead you into more effective ways of coping with depression when it comes. We are going to begin with the treatment of the basic element of depression and discuss generally its nature, its causes, its symptoms and its purpose.

Symptom

Now as we move into a more specific treatment of its causes, we are going to deal especially with depression as it relates to the nature of walking with God and with the Christian's role and expectations. Depression is: a symptom, a disease, a reaction. As a symptom, depression is part of your body's warning system calling your attention to the fact that something is wrong. The occurrence of depression with the disturbances of our endocrine system, with cancer, with a bad case of the flu, with a bad thyroid condition points to its symptomatic nature.

As a case in point, a number of years ago I went into a terrible period of time in my life when I actually thought I was having a nervous breakdown. I was so depressed that I could not stand in front of the church and sing and preach. This went on for weeks and weeks. I continued to get weaker and weaker. I lay in bed and cried day and night. Actually I thought I was going to lie right there and continue to get so weak that I would just eventually die at home. I was so depressed, worried, and full of fear that I could not even stand for my husband to leave the house long enough to get a gallon of milk at the corner store. I would cry like he was going to go to China and not come back for a year. It was a symptom of something that was deeper and come to find out after many tests, I had a thyroid condition—an underactive thyroid. The doctor told me that a thyroid condition in its worst stage could duplicate the symptoms of a nervous breakdown.

What I was thinking was "depression" and I was blaming myself for what actually was a physical condition. I thought that I was not a good wife, not a good preacher, and I was not being a good example for the saints. I was a mess, until I finally found the reason, the cause, and started to treat it medically with thyroid extracts. It finally began to level off and in addition to that I got "a hold" of God. The devil always latches on to a physical condition; he takes full advantage of it and squeezes every ounce of juice out of it that he can.

Sometimes you begin with a physical condition, or the symptoms of a physical condition, then as you get weaker the devil says, "HA" and ZAP—he's got you and you are down and out. Please be aware that you may not always initiate the depression voluntarily. It may come due to inadequate sorting of your thought patterns or some other area in which you could fail. It may be a truly physical, debilitating condition which, as a result of your body systems or any other disorder, points to a symptomatic nature.

In most severe forms, a psychotic depression is an illness in a category of its own—an entity in itself. That is a horse of a different color. You will have to recognize that there are physical, debilitating conditions that can cause a depression which can be worsened by the fact that one is not coping well with the situation nor taking steps to resolve the situation. Then it gets worse and the mental gears start to slip and then the spiritual gears start to slip and the first thing you know, you're a wreck and you don't know how you got there.

So let's go back all the way to the very outset and observe what happens. May I compare a psychotic depression, an illness entity all its own, to a kidney that failed to function which deserves and needs medical attention. If you break a leg, you go get it set. Now the mind, the brain, and the nervous system, which sorts all the data that goes in, can have the same type of dysfunction as the kidney, the heart, or the liver can have. It is also flesh that is supposed to operate in a certain manner and in some situations, those things occasionally get out of kilter. This is due to chemical imbalance within the body or some other biochemical problem. There are medical means of dealing with psychotic depression. This is not a bad ("bad" meaning "scornful or reproachful") thing to look upon.

I do know from my own personal contact with people and experiences that psychotic depression is an illness, an entity of its own just as a dysfunction of another part of the body is and it needs to be dealt with as such, and in the process alienated from spiritual things. Sometimes a chaining reaction will connect them to spiritual things, but we try not to spiritualize psychotic depression. They are two separate worlds.

And now, for our purposes, depression usually is a reaction to what is going on in life and more specifically to significant losses in life. This category of depression is the major group with which we have to contend daily. That is probably where we are going to dwell for the most part. Reaction.

Emotional

What are the symptoms of a depressed person? We are going to deal with three of them. The first—emotional symptoms. This seems to be the most painful and the most common. The symptom that most commonly characterizes our definition of depression is a low, sad mood. However, just as frequently, a loss of interest in one's environment is characteristic. These important symptoms can occur separately or together, but the more serious the depression the more sad effect is added to the loss of interest. There is a feeling of gloom, dejection, of moodiness. The person feels hopeless and may cry at the slightest provocation.

Women are especially susceptible to this. "Why are you crying? What did I do?" "Nothing." "Well, what's wrong?" "I don't know." There is a lot of negativity and resistance. If some one suggests going somewhere or doing something, the depressed individual is likely to respond, "I don't feel like it, I'm too tired." The thinking becomes slow and it even becomes painful to think.

The depressed individual cannot reason very well. It is extremely hazardous to make any decision when you feel you are depressed, ever so slightly. Contrarily, it is also hazardous to make important decisions when you are on an emotional high because you have a tendency to over-project that which you are able, within reason, to perform. You are just feeling great and you plan and plan and plan and then your calendar's full and you're over-obligated and you can't do it all. You're sinking and you can't meet it and you get this failing feeling. Then you get guilt feelings because you are not doing a good job. And then you are worn out and the chaining process keeps dragging you down, down, down, and it can be a tragic thing for you. So guard against making long-term decisions, very important life-affecting decisions, when you are either very low or high.

When a person is depressed, the person's mind is too occupied with the depression to do any extra work. A depressed woman can sit down and drink a quart of coffee, one cup after another, thumb through ten magazines, with dishes piled up to her eyes and laundry running out of the hampers. And she cannot figure out why she can't pull herself together to get up and get the work done.

You may be edging on one of these situations. When you are too preoccupied, especially with the depression or the thing that triggered the depression to the point that your mind is just going but your hands won't move and you're getting nothing done, you become very introspective and want to think and talk only of yourself.

Strangely enough, self-esteem drops. You would think that one who wishes to talk about themselves so much would have a lot of self-esteem, but they do not. They are lacking in self-esteem. And all of this dialogue about one's self usually is centered around questions as, "What should I do? Where should I go?" Everything has a question mark behind it.

Although everything is concerning the person and it is introspective, it is not a positive type of thing. It is a question, constantly not knowing. "Are you sure? What do you think?" But all the questions are inward. That's the sign you should watch for. Self-accusations occur. The individual becomes guilt prone and takes responsibility for everything that happens. Someone came up to me a couple days ago and very emotionally said to me, "I am so sorry. I have to apologize for so and so."

"Hey, wait a minute," I responded. "You didn't have anything to do with that."

The person had not done anything to cause the situation, but he was feeling guilt for it and apologizing for it. Sometimes we become guilt-prone. We take responsibility for everything that happens. But with this there is often indulgence in self-pity as well. We call this, "pity parties."

Most serious of all, death thoughts occur. Now listen carefully. This individual is not seriously contemplating suicide, but death is thought of as a way of escape, a way of getting out of all of this, a way out of decision making, a way out of facing the music, a way out. And it becomes a frequent thought and the more depressed the individual becomes, the more he focuses on that. The individual does not necessarily think that he wants to take his life (Most of us are too big of a coward to take our lives.) There's no way I'd have enough nerve to slash my wrist, just stand there and watch myself die. But when you are in a depression and you get low enough, suicide will come through your mind. This is the part of the picture that you need to watch for and if you see it popping its head up in your thought patterns too frequently, you need to steer yourself away from it. Don't allow yourself to dwell on those kinds of thoughts. They are not compatible with the Scripture, "Think on these things."

Physical

Now let's go to physical symptoms. These parallel the emotional symptoms and include a retardation of movement, loss of energy, sleep and appetite disturbance. Of course, these last two (loss of sleep and appetite disturbances) can go to both extremes. Either there is an escape into sleeping all the time or on the other hand there is difficulty in sleeping. The same depression in two individuals can take either route. One person doesn't want to get up; he doesn't want to wake up; he wants to sleep all day long. The other person can't sleep and becomes so weary because his body won't go to sleep. Therefore, it can be either. And there is difficulty in either.

Then there's the appetite. The appetite is depressed with the consequence of weight loss or there's a tendency to cope with depression by hitting the cookie jar too often, and eat, eat, eat and there we go! Bigger and bigger and *BIGGER!* You wonder where all of this weight is coming from. You did not realize that you were eating so much. It is possible to get into that syndrome with depression. The ultimate is weight gain. Then starts that chaining process—one thing adds to another. You start to put on weight, then you lose self-confidence. You look at yourself in the mirror, you feel inadequate, you feel "unnice." (Is there such a word?) You are clumsy, you're not your old self and that affects your mental attitude. It chains, and deeper and deeper you go into depression.

Perhaps one of the more severely depressed people will begin to neglect his appearance. The most common of all physical symptoms is a tightness in your neck or the pit of your stomach. Some men just let themselves go. When they really get into a deep depression, they don't want to shave anymore. They have a scrungy, scruffy, untidy look. Women are guilty of this too. In a depression you tend to lose sight of how you should look.

Spiritual

Then number three, spiritual symptoms. Again these may run into extremes. The most common is to pull away from God and to feel that God is rejecting you. We have a tendency to spiritualize our depressions. Try to remember that depression need not always be a spiritual problem. Just because you are in a depression does not mean you are having spiritual problems. You may be in "A NUMBER

ONE'' shape with God. You may be able to hit your knees and have a prayer meeting second to none and feel the glory and the presence of God and get up and walk back out into the living room and feel so low that the ants are crawling on top of you. Now you are asking, ''How can that be?'' Well, it *can* be. That's all I can tell you. You do not necessarily have to be on the outs with God to go into a depression or to experience depression feelings.

Somehow, in our circles, we always put that old spiritual tag on it and we say that if a person is depressed, bless God, they've failed somewhere. He must be committing sin or she's probably been running around on her husband because—and we start to add all kinds of weights on the scales saying that if a person is depressed then he is doing something wrong.

Transgression is a possibility, but remember that a depression does not necessarily mean there is a spiritual problem. Remember, you are a person, you are a human, you are a body, you are a piece of flesh that is meticulously put together and when something gets out of kilter, gets out of socket, one way or the other, it's going to throw you off balance. But that does not mean that you have failed God or that God is frowning at you.

Be careful that you do not spiritualize every emotion that you feel. Some people feel that God is rejecting them and then, as a result of that attitude, they began an actual spiritual withdrawal from prayer and reading. Less commonly, a person may become obsessed or preoccupied with spiritual things, spending long hours in Bible reading and prayer which is not done to draw closer to God but rather to escape from the world. This is regarded as a spiritual exercise. It is really a way of escape and it is a symptom of depression. When a person will stay on his knees for nine hours and not lift his head, he may be doing what we would call a "spiritual exercise." I can promise you that he is probably having some emotionally bizarre activities in some other areas of his life. I haven't found too many people who have nine hours to pray. Now I believe in prayer. I believe in long prayer. I believe in short prayer, too. But don't be fooled by a person who spends 12 of 24 hours secluded in a closet with a flashlight reading the Bible. That person may be experiencing depression or even some type of psychotic illness and he is escaping into the seclusion of *this* world to keep from having to face the *outside* world.

Major Categories Of Depression

What are the major categories of depression? There are three that I will deal with now. One is endogenous, the second, reactive, and lastly, neurotic.

Endogenous

Endogenous means "from within." These are the depressions that come from within our physiology and may be due to the disturbed hormonal system or nervous system. This could be an infection or some toxicity in the body. These depressions will often come in cycles. They can be aggravated by fatigue and stress and they do respond very well to antidepressant medication. I am not advocating tranquilizers, so please do not misunderstand me. As a matter of fact, I would discourage anyone from getting involved with tranquilizers. However, way out here in the margin we have to recognize the fact that there are some physiological disorders. Be sure that the illness is, in fact, just that before you get into that kind of thing. Don't forget, in the interim, that God still heals nerves as well as headaches and cancer. So, if your depression is an outgrowth of a physiological system or it is in fact endegonous, or from a source within, that you can take the problem to God in prayer and ask Him to heal the root cause of it. He can heal that as well as He can heal anything else. I am just recognizing sources; I am not advocating medication. In its severest form the psychotic depressed person could be categorized as endogenous; so it is a physiological malfunction from within.

Reactive

The second category of depression is reactive. These depressions are reactions to loss and are simply a form of grieving. That does not always mean death when I say loss and grieving. I am going to elaborate on the grieving process a little bit later. We have to come to terms with grieving as well as coming to terms with what we have lost in order for this to run its course and serve as well.

You say depression can serve me well? It surely can. It can make a better person out of you once you are more aware of its sources, its symptoms, its categories. Pinpoint it and see what the trigger is. Then let's learn how to cope with it to the best of our ability.

Neurotic

The neurotic depressions are lifestyle patterns used to cope with the anxieties of life. They do not involve a grieving process but a retreat from life itself. An escape. That third category of depression, *neurotic,* would actually cause a person to retreat into his or her own world, pull the shades down and forbid anyone entrance. Neurotic.

Does depression have a purpose? Yes, I believe that God created us to entertain this cycle which obviously comes to all of us at one time or another for very important reasons. It makes you feel better that something good is going to come out of it. Number one, it is protective. Depression can be protective. During a time of depression, you will find that you are, in a sense, removed from your environment. The primary symptom of depression is loss of interest. We have said that it is the "sad" effect that takes us out of our environment. We are no longer interested in what is going on around us. We seem to be somewhat withdrawn. We do not like to talk to have conversations with people. We just want to be quiet.

In the case of a disease, a depression that accompanies a disease can be also a protective shell that surrounds a person to conserve your energy and to keep you out of danger. Did you ever wonder why when you get extremely ill you do not want to see anybody and you do not want to talk to anybody? That is a form of depression. But God built that condition into your system as a protective measure, to conserve your energy and to keep you out of danger by virtue of the fact that while you are in such a weak, susceptible point, to be exposed to so much activity would be detrimental to your recovery. When you are down and you are sick and you do not want to see anyone, this very condition itself is a protective shield around you to keep you while you are in that weakened condition from being a recipient of things people would say to you, do to you, imply to you, when you are too low to handle them. Depression can be a protective measure that God has built in for you. In the case of reactive depression, it helps us pull back from things so that we can put things in perspective.

Depression is purposeful and protective. Unfortunately we have distorted the experience of depression. Most of us see it as something very negative and undesirable. That is not to say that all depression is justified. I believe that we can avoid a lot of the depressions that we go through. However, we grieve over the loss of things that we should not have had in the first place, things that we do not have and do not need—or just wish we had. We do not take care of our bodies; we exhaust ourselves. Look at our value systems, even in Christian circles. We don't differentiate between what is meaningful, what is important, and what is urgent. We always clamor over the urgent while the important sits quietly in the corner waiting for attention. We cannot tell the difference between that which is eternal and purposeful and that which is not eternal and is transitory. We get everything tangled up.

I wish we would learn to put little things in categories and build slots in our mind like a big mail box. All the things that come to you, take a good look at, pitch it into a certain slot. Eternal, put it in that slot. Not eternal, put it in that slot. Transitory, put it over there on the left and forget it for a while. Don't let something that's going to pass quickly get you down. Nobody's going to remember it a year from now. Why cry all afternoon about it? Let's learn to methodically divide our thoughts and therefore learn to get a handle on our emotions by properly categorizing those things which come to us.

Most Common Trigger: Loss

We can avoid a lot of depression by carefully analyzing what is causing our depression and coming to terms with those issues. By learning how to relate better to one another, we can avoid a lot of our depressions. Is there a common trigger in most types of depression? The most common category of depression in the reactive or central issue is "loss." Ninety percent of our psychological depressions are triggered by loss. It does not necessarily mean death of a loved one. Loss. It can be loss of control. It can be loss of self-esteem, status. There are so many ways that it could be triggered.

Real Or Concrete Losses?

It is possible to categorize these losses. Real or concrete losses. That kind of loss refers to the tangible things of life. That may range from breaking your camera to losing your loved one in bereavement or perhaps going through a divorce. It can be being stopped by the traffic cop and having to pay $25.00 for a fine. That's a loss! Well, your pride suffers and you lost $25.00. It is definitely a loss. Now those are real or concrete losses. However, they involve intangible things such as love, loss of control, loss of respect and such.

Abstract Loss

Obviously abstract losses often occur together with concrete losses.

Imagined Losses

The imagined losses are those which occur within our imagination, often entirely divorced from the facts of life. Suspicion. Imagining we are being neglected. Seeing two ladies talking. One happens to glance your direction and you are absolutely positive that they are discussing you. That's an imagined loss. You would be surprised how quickly you get a knot in the stomach. Imagined losses. Or you begin to imagine that someone does not love you anymore and you find out-of-context events to substantiate your assumption. You try to reach for pieces of the puzzle to pull it all together to prove you were right in what you imagined. Those are imagined losses.

Threatened Losses

And then, threatened losses are potentially concrete or abstract or even imagined losses. Threatened losses are very real but it is impossible to resolve them because they are only threatening at this stage. Discovering an unexpected lump in your leg may occasion a depression because of the threatened loss that is implied. You are already wondering whether the doctor will amputate it. It can be a damaging, destructive thing.

Loss Of Control

Now here is a fifth category. It is worth some consideration. It is loss of control in our multifaceted culture with so many forces controlling us. The loss of control with subsequent feelings of helplessness has become a very significant trigger of depression. As a result of this you feel like you are in a car driving, turning the wheel, and the wheel is not connected to the tires. You're turning and turning but the car is not responding. When you get no response, then you feel like whatever you're saying is falling at your feet and nobody's listening. As a result you start to give up. After the "giving up" process, the chaining process continues into the passive. And you see, the chain continues to go and it gets worse and worse. These are the most common triggers that cause depression.

IN THE MINISTRY

Does this topic seem a little strange? Perhaps you thought that to receive the Holy Ghost was to annihilate all depression. Somebody misinformed us. They said, "When you receive the Holy Ghost you will never be depressed again." That is not true. There are certainly greater measures to take and we do have some tremendous therapy that we never had before. However, having the Holy Ghost does not prevent a minister from going into or bordering on a depression.

Major Causes

What are the major causes? I would say that the very nature of the call of the ministry has to do with this.

Stereotypes

The ministry is a high and sacred calling and due to the very nature of its sacredness, we tend to ***stereotype*** what we ought to be. That is good as long as the pattern is cut after the Book and not after someone else. Of course, stereotyping after the Scripture is certainly permissible and advisable. You do things because the Book says you should do them. You look certain ways because the Bible says that is the way you should look and act. You change your lifestyle to adjust to what the Scripture teaches a Spirit-filled child of God should be involved in but you do not stereotype people. You do not look a certain way because that's the way the preacher's wife looks or that's the way the saints look or that's the way the preacher looks or the men in the church.

You need to get down to business with God and find your place in His Word and come by your own convictions. If there is a stereotype involved, it should be the New Testament believer, not someone who carries a name.

And so we get into this trend of becoming preoccupied as a result of unrealistic expectations hanging over us. We can become severely frustrated and ultimately depressed. People have actually backslidden and lost out with God because they did not come along as fast as they thought they should and had a struggle looking like the other women in the church right away.

I remember my mother saying that when she first got saved she had a "shingle bob." This was the way to cut hair in 1920 and 22. When she got the Holy Ghost and was around the old-fashioned Christian women with their long hair, she was seized with conviction. She had no idea what the Scripture said about hair. She only knew that she wanted to look like the other women! So she went out and bought a hairnet and she put it over her hair and rolled the excess net and twisted it around her finger and tried to pin it with what little bit of hair she could gather in the back to look like the other women. I have known people to actually lose out with God because they have become so frustrated in trying to look like other women so quickly. I'd far prefer that you look in the Book.

It is good to have examples, and I believe that you should have good examples to look to; even though the examples are there, your reason for looking like them should not be just to look like them, but because you matched what they look like and what the Book says and it is much the same. That's the reason you want to do it. So the depression that comes during this process can affect you if you do not handle it properly.

Lack Of Boundaries

Another depression-causing characteristic in the Christian is the lack of clear boundaries regarding what you are involved in. Can you ever live with the fact that there is no marker saying, "I have arrived. This is where I was going and I have arrived." It does not exist in your walk with God.

Paul also had those feelings. He spoke out of his heart in several instances when he said, "I press for the mark of the high calling in Christ Jesus." So the pressing makes me feel that Paul experienced some of these feelings that we experience because it's a job never done. It's a race never run. It's a walk never completed. It's a height never obtained. He said, "If I could just attain to it, but I can't relax—I just keep pressing every day." Due to the fact that there is sometimes a lack of clear boundaries and a sense that the work is never finished, that situation will set you up for new losses, particularly loss of control because you can't seem to get a handle on your feelings and relax about what is happening. Sometimes your self-esteem will suffer and if you are not careful you will go into depression.

Singleness Of Purpose

Another characteristic that tends to shape Christians is singleness of purpose. Our walk with God becomes a central force and that's the way it is supposed to be in our life, in everything in our life. You have to learn how to balance between your natural life and your spiritual life; otherwise you become so heavenly minded that you are no earthly good. So the singleness of purpose can throw you off track. However, your singleness of purpose is good. Your walk with God should be the central point of your life but you have to know how to handle that so that it does not depress you when you see things are not getting done. The result of this kind of thing is a loss of self-esteem and control which leads right into depression as a result of our notions of perfection.

Realism Versus Perfection

We are shaped by both internal and external forces that demand exceptionally high standards and there is that notion of perfection; expectation of perfection for yourself, for others—intolerance for imperfection. If you are not careful, compromise will happen and that will inevitably lead to frustration and then depression. You do not have the opportunity anywhere you go to be more involved to a greater degree and have opportunity for conflict and distress that can lead you to depression than when you are closely entwined in the church. It is especially hazardous if you are involved on a Christian school staff because you are rubbing shoulders with the same people seven days a week and five nights a week. So being people-orientated with the abstract losses that may be suffered in relationships, can be a specific cause for depression—conflict and interpersonal relations that go sour.

If we could ever learn not to be intimidated by strong-willed people who get pushy! Know who you are, what you are about, where you are going, not only where you are going but how you are going to get there. Purposes, objectives, and goals lay the door of your heart and mind wide open at all times for counsel and correction. Be very open, kind but up front with people; frank, but sweet. Try not to leave anything to misunderstanding or imagination or suspicion.

Spurgeon once said that simply being human means that we will minister God's grace through tears and perplexities and we will often be cast down. He also said that we sometimes abuse our bodies with improper diet, with inadequate rest and by over-stressing them, working long hours without relaxation. Days which God intended to be our rest days end up being hard days of toil. He said that if we do not take the time to rest at one point or another, then depression will ensue.

Spurgeon spoke these words many years ago. He reminded his students that Jesus Himself recognized the limitations of the human frame and in the midst of ministering to needy people He advised His disciples to go into the desert and rest awhile. Spurgeon further points out that the nature of the ministry will lead to depression. The passion of longing to bring people to Christ is never fully satisfied. That heavy load that is on your mind constantly, whether a minister or a layman with a terrific soul-winning burden, tends toward depression. Then if you are in a position of leadership directing and controlling large numbers of lay people within the organization, you will have many occasions for losses that may lead you into a time of depression. If, in fact, you understand this, you will be able to avoid depression.

Proneness To Depression

Who can share his burden?

Some of the proneness to depression in the ministry is due to the fact that the minister cannot share his burdens with anyone else. It is a fact that the minister's job is isolated and lonely for one of two basic reasons, either the minister feels that it must be lonely, or there is, in fact no one to share his burden with. In the first case the minister robs himself of the catharsis of sharing because he accepts the stereotype of the pastor as one of spiritual excellence and leadership and will not divulge the fact that he is experiencing the same problem and damage his credibility or damage his image.

Now recognize that I am going to be sharing some very deep and inner feelings involved in the ministerial function. Those of you who are not in the ministry feel them from the outside and pray for your pastor because the burden is very heavy. Hopefully when we finish this study you will have some understanding why he cannot divulge his problems because it will endanger his image, not that it is a selfish or narcisistic idea, but simply because it is not wise to do in every case.

Who understands?

In the second instance, it may be difficult for the minister to find someone who will be understanding, who will not be judgmental, and in either case whatever his reason not sharing his burden, the minister loses an effective buffer against depression when there is no one to turn to. He is really in a trap. He does not always have the advantage the layman has to vent his feelings and frustrations. Sometimes even his own companion does not understand.

There is a state of mind in a minister who carries a heavy load where it is a fact that *no one understands,* not even his wife who knows more about his problems than anyone else. It is a very strange thing.

Whom can he trust?

Then another consideration is, "Who can you trust?" Really, who *can* you trust with your inner thoughts, feelings, concerns, and doubts, if there are any? You don't dare vent those feelings. And you and I know that when you are in a depressed mood you have doubts about many things. It is better to contain those in your mind and try never to voice them, but most people go ahead and say what is on their mind and then they have to go back and say, "You know what I said, forget it, I feel better now." If a minister would ever voice any doubt that he had, it would wipe him out. He might as well close his book, resign his church and forget it. So he is really in a trap. He has no one to turn to but God Himself.

Depression An Occupational Hazard?

Can depression be avoided?

The occupational hazard of depression can be avoided. It absolutely can be avoided. Very carefully prepare for it and carefully analyze what is going on between yourself and other people, between yourself and the work. You can avoid depression, perhaps not all of it, but a lot of it can be avoided. Avoid depression by heeding the messages that are flashed out to you in one form or another.

Example: Some very tender, quiet, sincere individual comes and asks for your advice and before he hardly opens his mouth, you just blew him away, chewed his head off, and kicked him in the seat of the pants. He walked away crying and you know that you really fouled it up. You blew it by saying the wrong thing and hurt the situation more than you helped it.

Analyze the situation.

When you foul up just once, you had better take two steps back and take a good look at yourself. This goes for administrators, supervisors, and monitors when children come to you and you have not had the perception of the problem. The child is in a dilemma and you just run off the top and, as it were, slap him up against the wall, kick him down the hall and tell him, "Don't you ever come back and ask such a stupid question again."

You fail to see the problem and you fail to help. Take two steps back and look at yourself. You could be getting into a fringe area that you need to look at.

Heed the messages of warning.

Be honest with yourself. Depressions will send their little warnings out. Learn from your depression and use it as an ally rather than viewing it as an enemy. The greatest byproduct from depression is what you gain from God on your knees in the prayer room.

Learn from depression.

I have no reference but my personal one, so please pardon—I know my own experience. When I am at my wit's end, I have tied the knot, I am hanging on, my hands are tired, I am weary, I don't want to see anybody, I am sick, I don't want to hear another phone call, I don't want anybody to knock on my door, I have *had* it. When I get to that place I am no good to anybody or myself and I am dangerous. You better thank God that I go in and close the door when I get like that. I would do more damage in thirty minutes than I could fix in six months.

When you get into one of those moods or depressions or feelings or whatever you want to call that monster that knows how to grip you with all forty fingers and, like an octopus, wraps itself around you, go to the farthest corner you can find. Get down on your face before God, weep, sob, pray, and pray, and pray, and pour all that garbage out before Him. Tell Him how stinking, rotten, and mean you are and how much you need Him and pray yourself out of that mess and into the Spirit and then let the Spirit pray within you for awhile. The devotional tongue was not given to decorate your spiritual anatomy. It is a vital part of your being and existence. It is for a purpose. There are things that you can say to God in other tongues that you cannot utter in human words. It is to me the greatest therapy that one could wish for.

Use depression as an ally.

When I come out of the closet after a time like that, my soul is tempered. I could stand in the road and let the whole world run over me and never retort when just thirty minutes before I was ready to take them all on and box them to kingdom come. Prayer will take the fight out of you; it will take the nastiness out of you. It will take the gloom and despair and the hopelessness. You cannot come out of the presence of God and remain the same if you really pray in the Spirit. We learn to use these times, not as enemies and say, "Oh God, I feel horrible," but embrace that feeling. It is a time to pull yourself aside.

Just as when you get very ill and you don't want to see anybody, God built that into your physiology. When you are so sick that you cannot lift your head off the pillow and you don't want anyone to come in or call, God made you that way so that when you are low or down and out and very susceptible that you would have protective custody around you. That way you are not infiltrated by the things that would do you damage. So it is when you feel yourself in one of these moods or depressions or spirits, rather than lash out and fight and spit fire and carry on, recognize first of all, you are going through a process. Learn how to cope with it in an organized manner. Take a good look at the situation and recognize that you cannot handle it; be sure to get to the prayer room and retreat into that quiet time. Try not to talk to a lot of people when you are down and out because you are not going to say the right thing.

Four Categories Of Loss

How would you relate the four categories of loss to the ministry? Let us study concrete, abstract, imagined, and loss of control.

Concrete loss.

The concrete loss might be when you come before the church with a vision you have for a new building program and it is received very negatively. It did not turn out like you hoped it would. You had invested so much time (and probably money) and thought, you believe that it is what God wants for the church but you cannot help the low feeling that you get when you are not received like you thought you would be. That would be the real or concrete loss.

Abstract loss.

An abstract loss in the ministry may be illustrated by the loss of sense that people are actually benefiting from your ministry. If you rely on positive feedback every Sunday from those people who come around and say that was a really great sermon and you become dependent on that thing, then the Sunday when you think that you did the very best everybody just gets up and walks out—that's an abstract loss. And then you are wondering—what good did I do? So that experience can be depressing.

Imagined or threatened loss.

Then there are the imagined losses. They closely parallel this example. Perhaps a group that you have appointed called a committee (although I don't like the word committee—a camel is a horse that was built by a committee) and have not invited you to participate. They are kind of running ahead of you and there are things that you do not quite approve of and you begin to feel a little bit queasy and insecure with the whole thing.

Maybe you have projected that you are going to do something. You have voiced it, you have said, "This is what I am going to do in God's work." Then suddenly you feel that you may not be able to do what you have told everyone you are going to do. These are called threatened losses. Be careful there.

Loss of control.

Two areas of ministry relate to the fourth type of loss—the loss of control. I call it *learned helplessness and lack of assertiveness.* When ministers fail to assert their positions that they have been placed in, there is a sense of helplessness that can lead to depression. This is not prevalent in our area, but is applicable in districts where churches change pastors every few years. A 25-year old novice pastor, when placed in a church that has been in existence for forty years and although he's quite sure that the board is going to approve of him, he gets a little bit queasy. Conflict arises when his idea of the role he should be fulfilling will not fit other people's ideas or that of the former pastor. That leaves him in a state of helplessness and there is a loss either in not asserting what he should be doing or wanting to do that which is in conflict with others.

Losses: Ministry Related Or Philosophy Related?

Are these losses related more to the minister's philosophy or are they inherent in the ministry itself?

Stereotypes

Some are related to stereotypes of the ministry. Each minister has a philosophy of ministry, so we are looking at two things. We are looking at the ministry itself which by virtue of its nature contains certain philosophies. On the other hand, we are looking at an individual who is a minister and has his own philosophy of what the ministry ought to be. Two things: often we find conflict with a church's expectations so it is extremely important that you as a congregation are clear what your philosophy of the ministry is.

Keep ideals realistic.

A new preacher going into a church which is already established is especially vulnerable to frustration and depression because much of his philosophy is not explicit, very likely idealized. A young minister should set realistic goals—you should bring your ideals down to a realistic level and don't float in the clouds too much. You will bottom out as it were. Then you can begin a recovery process.

Depression Cycle

An ideal depression cycle for a relatively insignificant loss does not have to be longer than two or three days unless you resist going into the depression. This will abort the process which will lengthen the time you are depressed. The depression cycle—what is it? Something has triggered the depression cycle and what is it? Some kind of a loss. As a result of that loss you start down. Now that downward journey, bottom out, and back up need not last more than two or three days. That's about how long it takes for the whole problem to dawn on you good and proper. That is how long it takes for you to recognize all of the implications and ramifications of the situation, think it through, do some of the talking to people that are involved, and work on it or leave it alone, whichever happens to be the wisest for the time. Sometimes leaving it alone is far better than working on it. But this feeling of depression need not last longer than two or three days. It will give you time to read a lot more Scripture, spend a lot more time in prayer, and work yourself through what I am calling the grieving process because, remember, you lost something. The loss is what has triggered this cycle to begin. After the cycle starts, you go down, you bottom out, you pray through and you start back up and all of that should not take more than two or three days, unless you dig your heels in the ground and refuse to yield to the program. Do you get the picture?

Learn Spiritual Maturity

The program is designed to teach you lessons. It's designed to give you a new insight into spiritual maturity. It's designed to teach you lifelong lessons that you at some point in your future will be able to share with someone else and help them through the same type of dilemma. All things work together to them who love God who are the called according to His purpose. Do you believe that? It applies even to a two or three day depression cycle. So the next time you feel yourself starting down, stop just a moment; take a look down into the valley and wait for the trip back up and out. It will come if you will allow all of those things to transpire that God has built into the program. Included in them are the sermons and Bible Studies and Sunday school lessons on the very topics that are bothering you that nobody knows anything about but God.

God speaks to the preacher, God speaks to the teacher. When he or she gets into the pulpit or into the Sunday school class and says just the things you need to hear at that moment. You may be about two days old in a depression sitting at the very bottom and suddenly you feel yourself starting to come back up. But if you get frustrated with the condition, if you get disgusted with yourself, if you are aggravated with yourself or others that you may blame for causing it and you get a lot of outside interference involved in this depression, which is really your baby to spank (it doesn't belong to anybody else, so keep it off their doorsteps and off the telephone) then you handle it.

Let the grieving process take place. There is a loss so you are going to grieve. You have lost something somewhere. Analyze it, pinpoint it, figure it out, grieve over it, weep over it, go down, bottom out and come back up and let it happen. When you come out of it, I guarantee you that you'll be more spiritual, you'll have a closer touch with God, you'll have a better view of yourself, a more realistic opinion of what you can handle and cope with and God will be glorified in the victory. The depression cycle.

The grieving process.

Clinically speaking, the more fully we allow ourselves

to experience the loss and do our grieving, the shorter the duration process. Have you ever heard the comment about someone who lost a husband or a wife, let's say a wife for example. At the graveside and at the funeral she was just overwrought with grief and you just couldn't tear her away from the coffin. Let's say a wife for three days now has not stopped crying. She won't eat, she is just weeping out her very soul and when it's time to close the lid on the coffin, you cannot tear her away from her husband's body. She is just clinging to him and in order to close the casket the minister and his wife and the family have to literally tear her away from that coffin and drag her out of the funeral home. At the gravesite it is the same thing. She can't walk; she is so overwrought with grief and she is weeping and continues to weep for two weeks. Thirty days later she is looking a lot better. Three months later she's engaged and in four months she's married again. Then somebody says, "She could not have meant all that grieving. She probably had him (the new husband) on her mind when she was up there doing all the bawling."

Did you ever hear snide remarks like that? That is the furthest thing from the truth. That woman was able to weep her way through the process and come out on the other side a whole lot faster than the woman who stands there in a reserved manner, not wanting to cry and not wanting to make a scene and containing it all and then going into a depression, not wanting to see anybody or talk to anybody. She may be in a bad condition a year from now. The pastor and his wife will still be trying to pull her back into the mainstream of activity two years from now. Why? She clogged up the flow of grief. She aborted the grieving process and she will not get over the situation and let her grief and sorrow go until she pulls all the stops out.

The grieving process is a very real thing and even in the most minor kinds of losses, you have to recognize that cycle and allow it to take its course. The more fully you allow yourself to experience the loss and do your grieving, the shorter the duration of depression.

We have difficulty in doing this in our culture because there is constant pressure on us to short circuit the depression. You are told that you are failing God if you are depressed and you are not letting God do His work and all those kinds of things. These attempts may turn the depression cycle into a depression spiral. You know this well-meaning person who comes along and says, "Snap out of it, you're in the pits again." Such reaction may turn the depression cycle into a depression spiral where the depression literally gets out of control.

Depression spiral.

Now what are the components of a depression spiral? It begins when the ideal or the normal depression cycle does not complete itself and we begin to react to the depression itself. That's where the rubber meets the road.

We begin what I call an emotional chaining process, where feelings of guilt, anger-guilt, and self-pity are literally chained to each other adding their component of loss and intensifying the depression. Any one of those things could be volatile within themselves. Anger isolated from depression is dangerous. Guilt is dangerous within itself.

Self-pity.

Self-pity is tragic all alone. But when you link those three things with a depression and you start this chaining action, intensifying the depression, very soon you will find yourself in a deep dive with each of those abstract losses, giving an additional kick to the momentum. What was, in the beginning a small, insignificant loss, by this process of emotional chaining, puts you into a very deep depression. You see, the faster it turns and the shorter the radius, the more momentum that you gain this spiral process and then when you get there it makes the identification of the original loss very difficult. You have forgotten what even started the problem when you get down to that stage and the trigger is relatively insignificant at that point in time because the spiral has started. A depression spiral can totally incapacitate you. Be aware of those things. Try to avoid them.

Is Emotional Chaining More Of A Problem For A Minister Than A Lay-person?

I think so. Because the minister is driven by a set of higher expectations than the lay-person. While it is relatively easy for a lay-person to excuse their performance of a task in the church due to a lack of training, a lack of experience, or a lack of theological sophistication, the minister cannot get away with that. There is never any real excuse for the preacher, therefore emotional chaining does become more of a problem for a preacher than it does for a saint.

Model demands.

He often sends very clear messages to himself. He says to himself daily, I have to be better spiritually than anyone else; I have to be the role model; I have to be the model saint; I have to be the model father; I have to be the model husband; I have to do everything perfectly, flawlessly. The minister constantly tells himself this and so he quite easily takes on himself a set of unrealistic expectations. These high expectations lead to increased guilt because of the very fact that it is impossible for him to attain all of those ideals he has set for himself. Impossible goals along with the guilt feelings when the goals are not met begins the emotional chaining and that aggravates the problem.

Failure sense exaggerated.

There is a strong tendency for ministers not to have the courage to be imperfect or to make a mistake. I am not advocating that preachers be content being second-rate or less than the best. My point is that preachers have an exaggerated sense of failure which turns failure from a steppingstone to growth to a negative aspect of their lives, a punishment type of experience. You see, you can make a mistake sitting on the backseat of the church and nobody sees it. But the preacher makes a mistake sitting on the platform and everybody knows about it. The ministry is a very difficult place to be in. Added to this is the potential for loss of self-esteem for the minister, which is so much greater in work related issues. He may be more susceptible to self-pity when the congregation he has given up so much for turns out to be ungrateful, uncooperative or insensitive. All of these set a minister up for aggravated emotional chaining which intensifies the depression.

My friend, those are not just words. I know the feeling and I am aware of the fact that many who read this chapter are our church people. So forgive me for taking the liberty to expose my inner feelings. I know how it feels to work your fingers to the bone, to give everything you can give, to do everything you can do, working eighteen hours a day, helping anyone who comes to you for help, bending over backwards in every way and then somebody turns around and accuses you of being selfish or building a personal empire or pocketing the money, showing favoritism or using people and when you finish using them you are going to abandon them because they are no good to you anymore and all this kind of stupidity. I know the feeling that every minister who leads a congregation will go through at that time.

Avoid emotional chaining.

I have known of preachers who have made the mistake of becoming compassionate toward someone who had a problem and eventually became somewhat affectionate. Then they became emotionally involved beyond the limits of pastoral involvement, then that depression which follows has a very large spiritual connotation. This is called transgression. You have violated certain, important principles of your calling. You are experiencing a loss of your relationship with God. You are in the state of transgression. Get on with the program. Repent, confess, get right. You will be surprised how much you will feel better. The process is to allow yourself a normal grieving cycle, confession of sin, perhaps an apology to the person, before you can allow yourself to go through the process to come out a whole lot wiser than you went in.

Particular Times When A Minister Is Prone To Depression

There are particular times when a minister is prone to depression.

Monday: Post-adrenaline phase

A typical minister probably experiences the worst depression on Sunday afternoons or on Mondays. I have always said I wish that I could unplug my telephone and lock my doors on Mondays. Monday is the hardest day in the week for me to function. I never could really understand why until I began to delve and study and learn a few things. Now I understand why I feel the way I do on Monday. I still feel the same way, but at least now I understand it! Now I can cope with it a whole lot better in that I understand it. Most of us did not realize that the normal post-adrenaline phase of your biochemistry is in action on Monday, after you have given out everything on Sunday. Your adrenaline has just been going, going, going, going and just flowing and pushing and praying and singing and shouting and preaching and whooping and hollering and counseling and ripping and raring and tearing and dancing and then Monday morning—The minister who has been drawing heavily from the adrenaline flow is now experiencing a reaction which is combined stress, conflict, and depression.

Stress predisposes a person to intensified depression. Our physiology, exhausted from prolonged stress, simply does not have the reserves to sustain even small losses normally. Stress also has the tendency to make us less flexible which tends to increase conflict. When you are under stress you will break faster than normally. The very nature of a stressful situation makes you tense and therefore rigid and therefore more easily broken. So if you do feel stress in your life for one reason or another and you are not in the position to remove the source of the stress and you are called upon to kind of live in it or under it for a while, then this is the time you need to exercise extreme caution with whatever you do, whatever you say, whomever you associate with and how you allow burdens to be laid upon you. Loads that would not normally break you now could cause you to snap and explode all over somebody. Under other circumstances you would be very kind and compassionate. Stress is a very tricky thing and does very interesting things to our personalities. It alters our environment by changing our relationship to others. They will tend to be more guarded and sensitive when we are under a lot of stress, better known as "going out of their way to avoid you." They are not quite sure what to say to you because anything is the wrong thing to say. All of this increases the potential (there's that monster again) for loss and as a result of the loss, the grief and the depression. Wherever there is conflict there is a loss of relationships, a loss of love, a loss of ideals or some other loss.

Conflict arises from unrealistic expectations. (Let me elaborate on that briefly—people who are easily intimidated by other strong-willed people, people who do not know how to say no). Conflict arises from unrealistic expectations, inadequate assertiveness, poor group processes (which we know better as communication), and more critically from the manner in which we react to each other's demands.

Distress, conflict, and depression come early in life. The spiritual principles that come later are often difficult to integrate; therefore it takes a skilled person and a very complicated process to unravel all of those routes and help an individual understand and resolve these neurotic elements. So ultimately, as you are being counseled to help you through these times, the Word of God is a very important, if not the most important factor in resolving the problems of anger, guilt, self-pity, and pride. The Scriptures deal forthrightly, right up front, with all of those things. The Scriptures tell us how to handle all those things and what to do in those cases. You could in fact be your own therapist! You don't need to pay someone $60 an hour to analyze you and give you therapy when you can just read the Book and do what it says. That will be as good a therapy as you would ever get if not better!

Taking Time
To Communicate

Chapter 7

The Art of Questioning

One of the most crucial and valuable tools in the Christian worker's arsenal of communication skills is the art of questioning. The ability of a pastor, supervisor, or any other individual in a position of authority to ask the right questions at the right time is an essential and integral part of interactive management. Skillful questioning simplifies the manager's job because it gets the worker to "open up." The person involved feels free to reveal inner feelings, motives, needs, current situations, goals and desires. With this knowledge one is in a much better position to guide that individual to the ultimate achievement of personal, professional, and organizational goals. The bottom line benefit of this approach is greater operation, understanding and teamwork on everyone's part.

Questioning is a skill seldom taught. Even though questioning is an essential tool, there are few courses that deal with the fundamental principles of good questioning. Law schools may instruct students on productive ways to use questions within the courtroom where a witness has sworn to tell the truth. But these have little bearing on or pertinence to other situations. Outside the courtroom where people are not obligated to answer questions, a person must learn to obtain valid and useful information through skillful questioning.

Effective questioning is a skill that all Christian workers should develop. For pastors, supervisors of learning centers, and directors, it is an integral part of their job. The ability to ask the right question, to elicit crucial information, will greatly simplify your job as a counselor and/or problem solver.

Questions help people "open up." They give direction to someone who may not know how to begin. When people can "vent" feelings about a problem, you have a better idea of 1) how you can help, 2) whether or not the problem belongs on your desk or another person's desk, and 3) whether or not a "real" problem exists or if it is an offshoot of imagination.

When you and those you work with more clearly understand the situation at hand, your goals and objectives, you can both actively look for viable solutions that will satisfy the needs of the person, the church and the school. By using questions, you have a better chance of suggesting solutions that will enhance your mutual objectives.

No matter what you are concerned with you must know what kind of questions to ask in order to obtain the information you seek. This is really the most difficult part. It takes skill to know the right questions to ask. In addition to the actual information being sought, other aspects of questioning are:

1. How to ask questions (especially if they are personal),
2. When to ask questions,
3. Who to ask questions in order to get the most accurate information.

I will now consider three major sections:

1. Why people ask questions. (This will give you a better feel for how to use questions in different situations.)
2. Examine the different types of questions that can be asked.
3. Strategies and techniques. There are specific "how to's" of questioning.

PRINCIPLE: For questions to accomplish their intended purpose, (i.e. solving problems and/or finding solutions) the person being questioned must feel good about the process.

WHY PEOPLE ASK QUESTIONS

The first and foremost function of a question is to motivate communication. By asking a question, you open the channels of communication and begin a verbal interaction. (Did you ever try to hold a conversation with someone who "clams" up and won't talk or respond?)

Once the questioning begins and a line of communication is open, the function and nature of your questions may change. You will continue to motivate communication but you may also use questions as tools to gain information in other areas.

Questioning To Gain Information

Questions are used to ascertain facts about a number of things; namely, 1) the individual, 2) their personal goals and/or ambitions, 3) personal and professional problems, 4) motivations, and 5) performance levels.

Questions about all these areas may provide insight that will lead to a solution. By having a person state his needs, goals, objectives, problems and current situation, you get a more reliable view of his sources of satisfaction and dissatisfaction. By asking direct questions relating to the person's needs, you can evaluate needs and solutions.

EXAMPLE: Student (ninth grade girl) will not sit with other girls but sits alone. When asked "why" by lunch room monitor, there are tears and the girl is brought to me.

PROCEDURE: State some facts to orient and clarify:

1. You are eating alone.
2. You refuse to discuss it with your monitor.
3. You are crying.

Before I "plow" into her, I need to "gain information":

1. How long? When did it start?
2. Have you really tried to overcome it?
3. What seems to be the hardest?
4. Are you willing to try again?

Stop. Take time now to build confidence.

1. You have nothing to be ashamed of.
2. The other girls don't know your problem.
3. Would it help if you had one friend?

Questioning To Uncover Motives And Gain Insight

By skillfully using questions you can determine the person's frame of reference. Knowing the person's perspective can aid in determining the best way to present your suggestion.

It is imperative to understand the goals and motives underlying the person's perspective. If you are perceptive (discerning) and attentive, you will perceive these and by doing so you are able to assist them in forming ideas based on motives and goals.

Questions That Give Information

You want someone to know a fact so you present it in question form.

EXAMPLE: (negative)

(Parent who unmercifully beats children.)

Did you know that the doctor has the power to send the state to pick up your children if you are reported as an abuser?

EXAMPLE: (positive)

(Parent who cannot work because of health and children suffer.)

Did you know that you qualify for assistance from Social Security?

CAUTION: Beware of insulting the person's intelligence by making these "information-giving questions" seem manipulative. Avoid broad, unsubstantiated claims that you cannot prove or that attempt to placate (to soothe or satisfy—conciliate) the individual.

Questions To Obtain Employee Or Volunteer Participation

Occasionally you have people who are withdrawn and uncommunicative. It is necessary to draw them out and get them to participate in the conversation. "Closed questions" will be unsuccessful and time consuming. "Open questions" are helpful, but finding the right topic is more difficult.

PROCEDURE: Use your own experience and insight to build a "trust bond" and break down barriers, then proceed. First, establish the fact that you do understand, then be sure he understands. By getting the person talking and giving information, you will gain greater commitment to follow through a solution that you mutually discover.

EXAMPLE:

1. A "trouble maker" on the church/school staff.
2. A naive staff member who is being "used" by this person to run interference for her. (The trouble maker creates the balls, and sends the naive one out front to throw them.)

By getting the person talking (using questions) and volunteering information, you allow her to build her own convictions and approach the problem properly without feeling that she is responding solely to your demands or opinions. This prevents her leaving your office and going out to say: "Sister Trout said she is a rat, a sneak, a liar, a plotting, planning trouble maker."

Questioning To Check Understanding And Interest

Questions provide the critical feedback necessary to make sure that the two-way communication is on track. This feedback allows you to verify that you have captured the true essence of the individual's message—the feeling and content. In addition, it allows you to evaluate the person's feelings and understanding about your suggestions and message.

Use feedback questions periodically to make sure you are understanding the individual. Feedback questions begin typically with: "Let me see if I can summarize your major concerns," or "I understand you to say. . . ." and end with, "Was my interpretation on target?" or, "Does that accurately summarize the problem?"

By doing this you are communicating a number of very important things to the person. First, you are showing that you are making a concerted effort to listen. Secondly, you are proving with your actions that the person's message is important. Thirdly, you are confirming the message so that there is less likelihood of misunderstanding and bad feelings. On the other hand, you should periodically check the person's understanding of your message to make sure you have made yourself perfectly clear. (You will be misunderstood far too many times as it is!)

> **EXAMPLE:** A young woman comes to ask advice on accepting a job and moving away. I explain pros and cons and then proceed to forewarn of problems and areas of caution, naming them one by one, telling her how to avoid and react.
>
> My counsel is misconstrued to mean I do not approve.

Simply, asking, "Have I explained it to your satisfaction?" or "Do you fully understand what I've said?" gives the person an opportunity to voice any doubts or questions he or she may have at the time.

Checking the "interest level" is also essential. You may say, "How does that sound to you?" You will know from the response how and where you stand. You will know by facial expression as well as words whether it's safe to conclude the conversation or continue it until resolved. Occasionally a person will sit through a session and having never made himself clear and, worse, having totally misunderstood you. Questions will break down the walls and open doors. Questions serve to feel the pulse and check the temperature. The right question can bring a lengthy conversation that has been going in circles to a quick "head." When you ask the right question that pops the cork, or blows the gasket, or sends the temperature rising, you know you are on target. By monitoring the person's reactions as you ask questions, you can eliminate misconceptions in your own mind.

Monitoring response will prevent you from "laboring" a point and avoid boring the individual. Don't continue to emphasize a point after a person has agreed. You could fail to check the response and assume the reaction is unfavorable when in reality it may have been completely favorable.

Questioning To Start The Person Thinking

Amazing as it is, many people have never learned to think for themselves. They are always accepting the opinions of others and adapt their attitudes in vital matters without independently thinking the situation through. So many times I've heard, my husband, Brother Trout say, "They are not thinking."

Use technique (Questions That Give Information) to start the ball rolling.

EXAMPLE:

Fact 1: Brother Agitator plays both ends from the middle.

Fact 2: He takes pleasure in gossip.

Fact 3: He is a chameleon (wears camouflage suit so he cannot be detected as a trouble maker).

Fact 4: Brother Agitator uses other people to convey his gripes and complaints.

Fact 5: He is never seen in prayer room.

Fact 6: He always sits toward the back.

Fact 7: Weeping for himself and/or others is missing from his life and experience.

Fact 8: Brother Agitator uses other people—gets them stirred up with questions and half truths.

Fact 9: He never presents all the facts when he talks.

Fact 10: Brother Agitator is, in fact, the tare growing among the wheat, well rooted in many lives.

Hazard 1: The person you are counseling has confidence in him.

Hazard 2: They, themselves, are not too swift.

PROBLEM: Person number two (Brother Dumbo) sits down in your office to "confidentially" discuss his concerns.

Concerns: "Brother Agitator is a misunderstood underdog."

Challenge: Keep a firecracker from becoming a cannon.

Question: (Questions That Give Information type) Ask Brother Dumbo, "Are you aware of the following information?"

Fact: Brother Agitator spent two hours in my office Tuesday night seeking counsel on how to handle problems with you. Do you, in fact, go over to his house and spend whole evenings until late at night "running your mouth?" How often do you call him? What is the nature of your conversation? Would you consider these conversations as being what the Apostle referred to as "busy in other men's matters?"

By posing certain questions, you can get the person thinking. They will then figure the problem out for themselves instead of you having to say: "Brother Agitator is a trouble maker and so are you."

Good questions will often result in the person saying "I see what you mean" without questions literally getting answered verbally.

Questioning To Reach Agreement

By asking if the person agrees with you, you can judge progress and thus determine whether or not to proceed with the subject. Rather than proceed with a subject that will bring you to a dead end, it is necessary to explore the areas of agreement and disagreement before you continue with a topic. When you say, "Does that coincide with your experience?" you should allow the person time to reflect and decide if he is in agreement with you.

Manipulative practices that try to promote agreement through rapid fire questioning tactics are undesireable. Even if you gain on-the-spot agreement, the person may later regret his answer, withdraw from the commitment and even try to sabotage it. Underhanded tricks will break a trust bond.

Questioning To Bring Attention Back To The Subject

If you fail to hold the person's attention, a question will serve to bring his concentration back to the subject.

Questioning To Give Positive Strokes And Build Trust

Asking someone for his opinion is a tried and true form of flattery. It acknowledges his opinion, confirms his value, and requests his participation.

Questioning and Psychological Reciprocity

Applying this concept to the questioning, listening and communication process means that if you question and listen to someone, he will, hopefully, do the same for you when you speak. Both persons are winners when they open their minds and hearts to the communication process. If you do all the talking and very little listening, you will develop a habit within others to tune you out. Irony: ''The more you speak, the less you are heard.''

Questioning To Discover The Tension Differential

The tension differential is the gap between what a person is presently doing and what he would like to be doing—his goals and objectives in relationship to his current situation.

Unfortunately, many people live in a state of ignorant bliss, thinking at a conscience level that they are okay, when in a subconscience level they are not. Questions may help a person come to grips with his goals and objectives as well as his present situation. With clear perspective and insight, the person can choose a new course of action, if it is warranted, by examination of the tension differential.

Questions To Determine ''Style''

People are uniquely different in behavior, learning, decision, and transactions. Keep these differences in mind as you deal with people.

A good way to determine style: Ask questions that give them opportunity to project verbal, vocal and visual clues . . .likes. . .dislikes. . .strengths. . .weaknesses.

Chapter 8

Think With Discernment

In his book, *Make Up Your Mind About the Issues of Life,* Charles Swindoll wrote an old Persian proverb that sounds more like a tongue twister than it sounds like sound advice. Nevertheless, it bears listening to. "He who knows not, and knows not that he knows not is a fool; shun him. He who knows not, and knows that he knows not is a child; teach him. He who knows, and knows not that he knows is asleep; wake him. He who knows, and knows that he knows is wise; follow him."

These four types are found in every situation that you will be involved with. Whether business, pastoral, or otherwise. Just in day-to-day church activities and staff interfaces, you will meet all four of these individuals. They do not always wear badges. They do not introduce themselves accordingly. But somehow you will come to know which category they fall into. You will never have someone walk up and shake your hand and say, "Hi, I'm Donald. I'm a fool." But he will communicate that to you sooner or later, loud and clear. He knows not and he knows not that he knows not, so shun him. So how are we to know whom to shun, whom to teach, whom to awaken, and whom to follow?

Scripturally, the Holy Ghost has provided us with a tremendous asset, and the Apostle calls it discernment. Discernment is not an attribute of a Spirit-filled Christian which is to be used to pry into the privacy of other lives. Discernment is not something given us so that we can sneak up on the back side of someone and know what they are thinking about us or anyone else. But discernment is, as the Scriptures call it:

> *"But strong meat belongeth to them that are of full age, even those who by reason of use have their senses exercised to discern both good and evil" (Hebrews 5:14).*

Discernment is the answer to many of your frustrations. And I strongly urge you to pray for it. If you do not today have a very keen sense of spiritual discernment, then you need to check into the prayer room and start asking God to give it to you. You need it, whether you think you do or not. It will automatically make for you many decisions that you have assumed responsibility for making. Whereas if you have an inherent spiritual residence of discernment, you will not be bothered with a lot of the frustrations and wrong decisions that you have presently. Skill and accuracy in reading character through communication is one of the assets of discernment. The ability to detect and identify the real truth.

Discernment is a valuable trait in communication. You recall, God told Solomon to make a wish, any wish, and he could have anything he asked for. I find it interesting that after God giving this opportunity, the king responded to God,

> *"Give therefore thy servant an understanding heart, to judge thy people, that I may discern between good and bad" (I Kings 3:9).*

In Hebrews 5:14 the Apostle Paul said that discernment is a characteristic that accompanies genuine spirituality. Paul also wrote about this in I Corinthians 2:14-16. In Hebrews Paul referred to it as a mark of maturity.

Discernment gives one a proper frame of reference. A definite line separating good and evil. Discernment will act as an umpire in the game of life. Discernment will blow the whistle on the spurious. Discernment will reveal the presence of fakes and counterfeits. Discernment in your life will cause you to be particular about the things you do, particular about the things you say, about the friends with whom you associate. Because once you begin to discern between good and evil, then the art of communication becomes a very important factor in your life.

You realize that you not only communicate to others, you are often victimized by the communication from other people. So you not only give out communication, but you are a recipient of communication whether you like it or not. We all come under the fire or the gun of other people. By having discernment actively involved in your thinking spiritual input, along with lots of prayer and walking with God and spending time in His work and with Him in the prayer room this will give you an accurate base from which you can appraise most situations which will automatically exempt you from many of the frustrating problems you tend to become involved in through thoughtless activity. Activity minus discernment. Activity you get involved with without having looked at it real good. It is as particular as a pathologist peering into a microscope. It picks and chooses its dates carefully. Discernment chooses its friends carefully. It does not fall for fakes. It can pick them out most of the time. Discernment does not flirt with phonies. It does not dance with deceivers. And it does not kiss the counterfeits goodnight.

Discernment will clean you up and set you on your feet and virtually keep you ready for the rapture twenty-four hours a day. Discernment has beady little eyes that go out like radar signals, day and night, looking for potential problems that could cause you to lose out with God. Discernment works twenty-four hours a day. Discernment would rather relax alone in a prayer room or along a bedside or a sofa in the evening time with the Word of God than to go out and have a hilarious time with the gullible gang. You see, its from that Book that I have made reference to, that discernment learns to distinguish fools from children or the sleeping from the wise. Discernment will tell you which category most everything or everyone falls into.

I John 4:1 admonishes us that we should stop believing everything we hear. Quit being so easily convinced by mere words that are communicated to you from others. Be more discerning. A little pickier. A little more choosey in the kinds of thing you choose to believe. Unless you give this a lot of thought, you will find that you and I have a tendency to believe everything we hear. Discernment will prohibit this activity. Be selective. Think. Discern. Undiscerning love spoils and invites more heresy than any of us are ready to believe or receive.

The tactic of survival, when facing the flaming sword of the devil is discernment. Fasten the belt of truth tightly around you. The very thing that will help you do battle with Satan on a day-to-day basis will also strengthen you in your relationship with your friends and business associates. And so you have accomplished two things: you have cleaned up your thinking process, you have become more selective in the things you believe and receive in your mind, thereby rejecting a lot of junk. And by so doing, everything comes out with more clarity, and life is not nearly as frustrating when you throw out the garbage. Did you ever clean up a closet or a room and take out two trash bags full of garbage and you looked at that and you said to yourself, "I don't know how I lived with this so long!" That is a picture of your mind. Discernment will clean out the closet. Discernment will get rid of the trash. Discernment will give you clear-cut standards by which to think, respond, and receive.

"A Christian worker without discernment is like a submarine in a harbor, plowing full speed ahead without radar or a periscope. A preacher, a teacher, or a Christian worker without discernment is like a loaded 747 jet liner trying to land in a dense fog without instruments or a radio. Lots of noise, lots of thrust, a great deal of power, and good intentions until it crashes. And I don't have another Persian proverb to describe the results."

It's disastrous. Who really needs a word to describe what happens when a person with no discernment becomes involved in a staff, in a pastoral position, as an evangelist in another man's church, etc. So you understand the very vital role of discernment in your thinking. Discernment is what happens in the *mind* as a result of what happens in the *soul.* Discernment is not in the heart and soul alone, but it rises up from the heart and soul and it infiltrates the mind and it influences the thinking and it sorts. It sorts and it organizes. That's what discernment does for you. I have seen it happen with disastrous regularity. People who had no discernment, no perception, and the problems were constantly erupting here, there. Put the fire out here, it pops up over there. If somehow as a Christian worker, you can bring this facet of spirituality into strong influence in your life, you will minimize the problems that you cause other people.

You would like to have some but you don't know where to get it? They don't sell it at K-Mart, and if you check the Sears catalog I don't think it can be ordered through Sears or Penneys. But, I will tell you where you can get it—on your knees. James 1:5 says, "God will give wisdom to those who ask for it." Go to your knees. Pray for it. Secondly, go to the Word of God.

> *"Thou through thy commandments hast made me wiser than mine enemies, for they are ever with me. I have more understanding than all my teachers: for thy testimonies are my meditation. I understand more than the ancients, because I keep thy precepts. I have refrained my feet from every evil way that I might keep thy word" (Psalm 119:98-100).*

Discernment is found in the Word. Thirdly, go to the wise. Proverbs 2:1-5 tells us that discernment is better caught than taught. Those who have the disease are often contagious. You can actually learn from other people how to be discerning. And this offer that God makes for us is for life and it comes with a satisfaction guaranteed clause. And anyone may apply for it.

So all of you, those of you who thought you would never be the one to be involved with discernment, I would like to tell you that you are a candidate and I strongly recommend that you get involved, actively involved with discernment in your life. Even those who think they know it all and know not that they know not can have discernment.

Take time to communicate. "Eight words are brashly smeared across the dashboard of a speedboat tied up at the gulf shores, Alabama. They reflect the flash and flare of its owner whose fast life is often publicized in sporting news across America. In off seasons the speedster resembles a shipless, beachcombing drifter with his stubbled beard, disheveled hair and darting eyes, rather than one of the highest paid quarterbacks in Oakland Raider history. If his profession doesn't fit his looks, his nickname certainly does. They call him "Snake." As swift and sneaky as he is on the field, Ken Stabler knows one speed—full throttle. So we shouldn't be surprised to read the saucy sign on his dashboard in his speedboat that warns all passengers when they get in. The sign says, "Get in, Sit down, Shut up, and Hang on."[2] I told Brother Trout that we should have a sign like that made and put in the front office, on the front door on his desk because it sounds like the motto that Brother Trout and I live by. If you want to be a member of this church, get in, sit down, shut up, and hang on. They tell me that if you plan to ride with "Snake" Stabler you should be ready for one sustained roar during the trip, because somewhere inside of him is an itch that hasn't been scratched. It is apart from the scream of that engine, and the blur of salt water waves rushing at the tune of eighty plus miles per hour. So once you get in and sit down you have a distinct feeling that shutting up and hanging on comes naturally.

Once you've committed yourself to such an accelerated velocity, nothing short of survival really matters. All that's o.k. if survival is all you're interested in. However, if the things that make life rich and meaningful to us and those traveling with us, involve more than survival, then speed is an awfully thin wire from which to hang. And so, I think it's important that we take the time to communicate with those who touch our lives on many levels.

In other words, if you really want some things to count, if we genuinely desire some depth to emerge, some impact to be made upon some life, some shadow to cross someone's path, whether it's your own children, your wife, your husband, your schoolmate, your roommate, those students placed in your jurisdiction, those people that you pastor, if you want to impact their life with truth, then there are things that matter, things that are more important than speed. It's essential that from time to time we slow down and communicate. Sometimes we have to stop completely. Just bring everything to a screeching halt and communicate and think and think and think. Now, not later. Not after it's too late. Not after the damage is done. Not after the soul is destroyed. Not after the family quit, left the church. Not after the young man gave up, backslid. Or the young lady felt that no one really cared. Let's stop now. Let's slow down long enough to communicate. Take time. We do not communicate on issues left neglected, too often neglected because we are so busy doing things that we can do without having to communicate.

My best reference is my personal frame of reference. And I know that it is my tendency to attack the list of things to be done today that I can do independently of communication with other people. That's my preference. And I have to put a harness on myself, a bit in my mouth, and yank the reign really good, and say to myself, "You've got to stop. You must slow down and take the time to do the responsibilities that require communication with other people."

My personal inventory reveals I will do first those things that I can do alone. If the task requires communication, maybe a staff meeting, a conference, a phone call—receiving or making one, a letter, a memo, a session seeking counsel from my husband before I make a decision on an issue, or a session seeking his counsel asking him to make a decision so that I can go back and communicate that decision, I will invariably put those kinds of things off as long as I can. So now you know my weakness. I am working on that weak area of my character development. And I have also discovered a major secret as I have begun work in this area. And that is "Living above my circumstances rather than living below them."

Some specific areas of frustration that I personally must continually watch and I'm sure you aren't a lot different than I am. They are: 1. Attempting too much at one time. 2. Unrealistic estimates. For example, not allowing enough time to do what I have assigned myself to do. As a result of that always running 10-15-25 minutes late because I did not plan enough time to include the unexpected phone call or the emergency situations. 3. Procrastinating. 4. Lack of specific priorities. 5. Failure to listen well. 6. Doing it myself. 7. Failing to delegate. 8. Unable to say no, no, I will not do that. No, I cannot do that. No, there's not enough time. No, no, no. Learn how to say no, nicely. 9. Perfectionism is focusing on needless details. 10. Failure to write it down is to forget it as far as I am concerned. 11. Reluctance to get started. 12. Absence of a self-appointed deadline. We love to give other persons deadlines, but we just don't always give ourselves one. 13. Doing first things first. My final comment on all of that is, do what you *have* to do, then you can do what you *want* to do.

FOOTNOTES

[1]Charles R. Swindoll, *Make Up Your Mind On the Issues of Life,* Multnomah Press, 1981, page 13.

[2]Ibid., p. 46.

Chapter 9

Evangelism In The Classroom

QUALIFICATIONS AND TECHNIQUES OF THE EVANGELISTIC TEACHER

With all the emphasis on adequate facilities and tools of teaching, we may have overlooked one of the most beneficial tools of all—the teacher that is in tune with the Holy Spirit.

Immaculate Perception

I have known a few people who made pretensions to the gift, but they were singularly obnoxious. You know the type. If you mention you heard on the news about so and so, this individual knows all about it—knew it three weeks ago, in fact.

We need not worry about perversion of true immaculate perception. In its most beneficial aspect, it is a providential gift and it seems to me that we teachers are the most logical and receptive persons for it. After all, our direct pipeline to omniscience almost demands that we possess "immaculate perception" of some kind.

Finders - Weepers And Losers - Keepers

Jesus said:

> *"For whosoever will save his life shall lose it: and whosoever will lose his life for my sake shall find it" (Matthew 16:25).*

The person who is willing to abandon himself to a burden for the souls of children will indeed find results in the altar. Weepers, in prayer, will be reapers in the altar. Losers of their life will keep, in the end results, life eternal; not only for themselves but for the children they evangelize. When you win a child you save a soul *and* a life.

Feed The Lambs - Not The Giraffes

Cumbersome jargon and the use of multisyllable words are often only a mask for the shallow and superficial thought. To feed every child in your class, *study deeply* and *teach simply.*

Our emphasis must be on *intent* rather than *content.* We spend so much time on crafts, room decor, visual aids, and other tools, that the emphasis may be inadvertently placed on the successful use of these items rather than their intended results.

Lest I be misunderstood, let me go further. Sermons for children must have *Biblical content;* however the tool of imagination must be coupled with the Biblical truths to produce desired results. The "profound" discourse, however convincingly delivered, will not produce the desired results with our "intent" interwoven into its fiber. Call it what you will. The worst they can say about you is "tear jerker" or "scare tactics." The proof of your delivery will be seen in the revival it brings—or the failure thereof.

There are times when the preaching (evangelistic teaching) must emphasize Apostolic Doctrine. Fine; but even then let the child evangelist use imagination in presenting the material. I believe in the conviction of preaching to children God wants something to happen in the hearts of children while the teacher is delivering the Word of God.

The child's mind is not a debating chamber. Options should not be part of the presentation, except in the case of positive versus negative. One given the choice between two roads cannot make a wise decision—if he makes one at all. Relative to doctrine there are no choices. State the doctrine clearly and simply—time after time—and you will indelibly imprint it on the students' minds forever.

In a class of young people, especially Junior High, a clear sound must be given. The only options Jesus gave was between the "straight way-narrow gate" and the "broad way-wide gate." Salvation has never been obtained using the multiple choice technique.

Confrontation

The prophet did not approach David with a lecture, complete with charts, on Levitical sacrifices. He simply told the king a story about a stolen ewe lamb and he reached the king's heart.

Nicodemus wanted to know about eternal life but Jesus talked to him about "birth." The woman at the well wanted to discuss religious differences, but Jesus kept talking to her about her thirst and God's living water.

PRAYING WITH CHILDREN

Pray *With* Not *For* Children

Youth, as a whole, finds prayer uncomfortable. They generally do not do it and have serious questions about its worth. They claim they don't know how to do it and many will feel embarrassed about attempting it.

As you begin to pray with children you will notice three stages:

Stage One – SNICKERING

For some strange reason prayer time becomes the comedy hour for some children. In spite of teacher's frowns, glares, threats, and thrashings—some children cannot keep from laughing, especially when the local Pharisee is praying for every missionary from the North Pole to the Equator. . .and purposely refuses to quit. That is until she has prayed for those who despitefully use her.

Stage Two – THE CYNICAL CYCLE

This is a tough one to pierce through. With an air of psuedo-sophistication, certain children (especially Juniors) will say by their actions, "What's the difference?". The Junior High years abound with these maverick thoughts. The whole scene of kneeling down, bowing heads, closing eyes, and praying for a "Holy Ghost," they neither feel a need of or want, is ridiculous to them.

Stage Three - GETTING PAST THE "PREACHER PRAYER"

This one is difficult to handle because it usually comes from well-meaning lips, out of sincerity and a desire to prompt obedience. We are tempted to preach to children, rebuke an unruly student or very subtly reinforce our own piety. Teachers can easily fall into this manipulative technique, since it is impossible to be interrupted in prayer. The temptation of taking this same liberty in the pulpit, before a captive audience, seems irresistible.

After passing through these three stages, however, we begin to realize the importance of proper technique in praying with children. The perfunctory uttering of meaningless, repetitious cliches that become boring even to God is of no value. The Lord Jesus thundered warning after warning against the empty verbosity which characterized the Pharisees.

Keep It Simple

You do not have to pray around the world three times or highlight every acquaintance between the poles and all the ships at sea. God is watching the heart—and that's what He responds to—not totaling up the verbiage.

Is your altar time losing its punch? Here is a way to find out. When the service is over, check the results. If it's good, GREAT! If it's zilch, sit down with your pastor and ask why. You have got a lot more to be concerned about than numbers.

The Key

The key to praying children through to the Holy Ghost

is to be able, by the help of the Holy Ghost in your own life, to determine whether the child is weeping because they are afraid, or if they are genuinely moved on by God. If the child is truly moved by the Spirit of God, it is only a matter of moments before they will receive the Holy Ghost because children are very credulous. They will do exactly what you tell them to do. They don't ask questions. They don't doubt. They can be led easily into a situation where they can yield to God. Of course, the key to getting anyone through to the Holy Ghost is to transmit faith to them and get them to yield. A child will do that very easily. But you have to determine whether they have been "scared" in a sermon or if they are under the conviction of the Holy Ghost. If they are under real conviction, they are seconds away from the Holy Ghost. If the person praying with them knows what they are doing they can get them through very easily.

Play Now - Pray Later

To relate effectively to children in the altar, one must relate to them outside the service or classroom. When you work with them at the altar you will not appear to be the supernatural, high and lofty, unapproachable saint if you have a good relationship outside the altar or classroom. You must gain confidence in daily living before you enter into the realm of supernatural with them so they will have confidence in you and trust your leading. Play now - Pray later.

PREPARING THE HEART TO RECEIVE

Stories

Jesus the greatest teacher of all time simply told stories.

He talked to them about things they knew about. He talked to Amos about picking fruit because Amos was a fruit picker. He talked to the Disciples about fishing and the woman at the well about water. He will come to where you are. The art of teaching is leading people from the *known* to the *unknown.* God starts with us where we *are* and then leads us to things we don't know about based to what we *do* know about. He used the parable of the fig tree because people knew about the fig tree. He elaborated and extended that knowledge to the unknown. The mustard seed, the wind, etc. These are things the people knew about. He took them from the known to the unknown to open their mind's understanding to spiritual things that they could not have attained unto unless they had the foundation or the platform of the mustard seed, the wind, or the fig tree. That's what He did. He was the Master Teacher. All good teachers do this—taking you from the known to the unknown.

The Value Of The Word Of God

The Scripture proclaims that it is "sharper than any two-edged sword." Despite all the visual aids and advanced programming we have in teacher's training there is one outstanding factor that is indelibly engraved in my life and that is this:

The Jews in ghettos and caves had nothing but the Word of God and they taught it in the most undesirable settings. They have by doing so, preserved a civilization, a nation, an ethnic group, and a religion for thousands of years. This preservation was accomplished by one active ingredient—the POWER of the Word of God, not experiencial association, but by the Word of God, alone. That's all they had.

They have taught that and only that in the most undesirable settings. They have preserved a nation, a religion, and a culture. Against insurmountable odds they have done it. That is one of the most outstanding things in all the world to me.

There is an inaccurate concept among many home missionaries. Some of them think they cannot do this or that because they don't have rooms, do not have carpet or decor, but remember the Jews made it without all that. They do not even believe in Jesus or have a Holy Ghost experience with God. They survived solely on the Word of God. Don't fall into the trap of depending entirely on a lot of programs and highly intellectual presentations, gimmicks, and gadgets, much of which is over the children's heads. Just the simple teaching of the Word of God and a burden for their souls is a powerful tool in evangelizing children.

The key to reaching a child is to remember that you can fool an adult, but not a child. Psychologists say that if a man, though held in disdain by adults, counted as offscouring and refuse in that locale, is loved by children you can mark it down, there is something good in that man's heart. Children know; adults do not always know. Children are drawn to goodness and purity. A child knows if a teacher loves them. They also know whether he has a burden or not. Children know if the parents are living for God or not, too.

A teacher who has a burden to transmit the Word of God to children's hearts is absolutely invaluable in a Sunday school. They are the ones who "get it done." Not the talented ones, not the ones that are clever with their hands; but the one who has a burden to transmit *Truth* to a child's heart. These are the teachers that mold people's lives.

The Transition Ingredient

How does a teacher move out of a lesson into the altar service? The only way it can be done is if your lesson has had spiritual content and that spiritual content moves the hearts of the children. The altar service will flow automatically from the conviction of the Word of God. When the children begin to pray (or seek) you can watch for the sincere ones. If you are perceptive you will be able to tell which children are genuinely moved on by the Holy Spirit. Once one or two are moved upon, others will follow suit. Children are very peer conscious. They will do what their peers do. They will not ask questions; they simply do it. They believe.

One difficulty should be considered. If you have a child that has come from a bad home environment where there is gross immorality, a lot of drunkenness, the child will have picked up a spirit and a complex personality with fears that he cannot escape in a Sunday school room setting. These children are difficult to reach because of the walls and barriers around them. But the average child who comes from the typical home is very easy to reach, especially the children of our own people.

Instructions To The Young Seeker

If the Sunday school lesson has not transmitted to them the understanding of the need for repentance, or a basic definition of repentance, repentance should be explained briefly. (Assuming we are praying with children who have attended for some time—at least two or three weeks.) Most children will understand these expressions because they have wept and repented to parents and had to ask forgiveness of brothers and sisters. If a child has a basic concept that they must do this with God then it is only a matter of teaching a child to yield to God or give themselves to God.

Have the child close their eyes and think—use the word "think"—about God. If you use the words "fasten your attention" they may not understand that. To say *think* means to picture Him in their minds. Let them raise their hands as a kind of surrender, a giving up of ones self. Tell them to worship the Lord. Explain that when they do receive the Holy Ghost, they will not speak in English. They will speak in a language unknown to them.

If you work with that, the moment you hear them begin to lose control of what they are saying, encourage them to let their tongues go and yield to what they feel. They will automatically begin speaking with tongues.

Dealing With Insincerity

The best way to stop a child from anything is lack of attention. If you discontinue your praying with a child that is insincere and say, "I am going to help someone else," they will voluntarily stop praying. But if they are sincere, they will continue to reach for God whether you are there or not because what they feel inside is automatically toward God and they will continue to seek for Him.

Growth Principles

It is easy to disciple children in a Sunday school setting. There is a way to live to maintain the touch of God. The class is the ideal place to do it. If you use Centers of Interest, a special group or center may be used to teach growth principles. However, you will not find as much difficulty in getting children to live for God as you do adults because children do not have the pressures of the secular world. They may have pressure or problems with brothers and sisters, but they don't have to worry about losing a job.

Children Praying With Other Children

Observe to determine which children have a special burden for other children. Announce a class for people, including other children, who are interested in helping children become saved. Teach simple things of believing; that it is not a time to laugh or look around but a time to pray and be sincere before God. The important thing is to teach them to help the person they are praying with to yield to God. It is easy to get children through to the Holy Ghost because they believe. They are credulous; they do not doubt or question. They do not rely on logic, reasoning or comparison.

Spurgeon believed that every person who ever eventually got saved had an experience with God as a child. Somewhere he has heard or felt the voice of God. They don't doubt when they "feel" God as an adult will.

Jesus said, "Unless you come as a little child"—that doesn't mean to toddle or fall over yourself on the way to the altar but to come emotionally as children come. Not foolish or playful; but gentle, obedient, truthful, pure, and trusting.

SUMMARY

Unless our children are evangelized, everything else we

do for Him will become an exercise in futility. Their spiritual lives will reflect our examples in prayer and consecration. It is true that "like begets like"; and if we are evangelistic in our soul winning, they will be soul winners.

Jesus proved His love for little children when He reproved His disciples when they wanted to send a group of children away. Jesus used the opportunity to teach on who would enter the Kingdom of God. God has used children to accomplish His own high purposes because of their simple trust: David the Shepherd boy, Josiah the boy king, Samuel the boy who heard the voice of God, and the lad who trusted Jesus with his loaves and fishes.

Children are pearls of great price, invaluable to the work of God. Let us not overlook this great Army. When a child receives the Holy Ghost an *entire* life has been preserved from drugs, alcohol, immorality, and the vices of this world. The only escape for our teenagers is the Holy Spirit, alive and real in their lives, implanted there by a Sunday school teacher who had a burden for them as a child.

Qualifications and Techniques of The Evangelistic Teacher

Chapter 10

The Need For Communication

PRIMARY PURPOSE

The need for communication. Its primary purpose is to prevent isolation and promote involvement.

ELEVATORS

Elevators are weird places, aren't they? Did you ever notice? Did you notice how people act in a crowded elevator. You are crammed in there close with folks you have never met. So you try real hard not to touch them. Capacity is listed at thirty and there are forty-five people in there. Occasionally you hear someone say, "Excuse me please," or "I'm sorry," when somebody gets their toes stepped on. But you don't look at anyone in an elevator.

Oh, no! You just watch the numbers. That's all you look at. They go on and off and the floors change and you just stand there and look at them. People who are about the same height, on an average about the same build. Most of the time they speak the same language but they are total strangers. Nobody mutters one thing to anybody else. Everybody is suddenly dumb. Silent as a bunch of nuns, just nothing. It's almost like there's an official sign hanging on the wall that reads, "No talking! No smiling! No touching! No eye contact allowed!"[1]

"That elevator is a microcosm of our world today. It's a very large, impersonal institution where isolation and independence is the order of the day. The basic quality of our healthy social lives is being diluted. It's being destroyed, it's being distorted and demeaned by the elevator mentality."[2] It can even creep into the college or the church. Unfortunately, the elevator mentality creeps into the home and the marriage. Nobody talks to anybody, we just stand and watch the numbers. What's the date? What time is it? These are probably the two most important questions asked all day long. Elevator mentality. What floor are we on?

This tells me that we as a rule are really out of balance in the area of communicating with people. Anyone who tries to communicate is considered fresh and the rule of thumb is, don't smile or they'll think you're up to something. If a young man is friendly with another young man, he's considered to have been propositioned. If a young lady is half civil and nice, she's considered to be flirtatious. I understand why things have deteriorated in our society to that point, but I think there is a place somewhere that we as Christians can emanate from our beings pleasant personalities, the Spirit of Christ. We can communicate with each other on an, "I care about you" basis without getting mushy. And conversely without being so cold that nobody wants to talk to us.

We see ourselves as victims of a society where the rule is, no hassle, no talking, no eye contact, no communication, no conflicts, no involvement, no accountability, no need to share, and no need to reach out or care. Just stand and watch the numbers and don't look at anybody.

ISOLATION

Dr. Philip Zimbardo, who is a professor of psychology at Stanford and is also the author of one of the most widely used textbooks in the field, addresses this issue in an article recently in the magazine, *Psychology Today*. The article was entitled, "The Age of Indifference." He pulls no punches as he writes. And I quote him,

> "I know of no more potent killer than isolation. There is no more destructive influence on physical and mental health than the isolation of you from me and of us from them. It has been shown to be a central agent in the etiology of depression, paranoia, schizophrenia, rape, suicide, and mass murder. Isolation or indifference. The devil's strategy for our times is to trivialize human existence in a number of ways by isolating us from one another while creating the delusion that the reasons are time pressures, work demands, or anxieties created by economic uncertainty. By fostering gnosticism and the fierce competition to be number one."

The only escape that I see from what he terms indifference, is *communication.* Think of people as a valuable resource. Think of individuals, people, your roommate, your dorm supervisor, your learning center supervisor, your pastor, your director of Christian Education, your music director, your friend, and at work your boss. People, people, people! Think of people as being a valuable resource for you. You can learn unbelievable things from people. If you will be selective and if you will be aware of those who have certain attributes or qualifications that you deem to be desirable. Attach yourself to them ever so silently, even without them knowing it, and observe them. Make notes of their activities. Observe their decisions. Note how they handle certain situations. Create for yourself out of these people a valuable stockpile of information.

The young men that have aspirations of pastoring a church should have one notebook with nothing in it but notes of your observations of your pastor or wherever you happen to be at the time. You will learn so much by observing. Observe how he handles a service. Observe how he handles a situation. Things that are not necessarily cloistered or private or confidential. Things that are in the open for all to see. Observe the way he conducts a service. Observe how he handles a disturbance in a service, something that is a little out of the way or sort of off the beaten track in the normal course of events. Take a mental note of what was done, what you saw being done, what was said. Say, "This is the set of circumstances, and this is what I observed taking place." People are a valuable resource for learning.

You can actually devise for yourself an education by extracting from others, learning in various situations. If you will just wake up, and decide that you are going to listen and observe. I would refrain from a lot of discussion about it. As a matter of a fact, I would keep it very private. Don't let anybody read your notebook. But *use people as a valuable resource.* If you come to me with a problem and I give you a certain decision or an answer, go away from that conference and sit down and say, "This was the problem and these are the facts." Record to the best of your ability, the things that I said to you, and my reasons for saying them to you and the lesson to be learned in it all. Should the Lord tarry in a few years that diary or that resource book will provide for you some things that you can go back to and draw wisdom from because it won't be too many years until you may be in a chair where you are giving advice, you are answering questions and if you wait until the questions are asked of you to start learning, you are going to have problems.

ESCAPE FROM ISOLATION

People are your most valuable source of information. Work hard at communicating. Establish meaningful relationships where communication is not a matter of business or convenience but it is necessity. We must come to terms with all of this. We absolutely must come to terms with it. The need for positive, effective communication on all levels, at every front is urgent. Jesus gave us the ultimate example. He provided for us a tremendous pattern that we can follow. Jesus did not isolate Himself in a pulpit. His philosophy was not, "Do as I say, don't do as I do." Jesus not only preached but He *cared.* He *reached out for peo-*

ple. He listened. He cooked. He baked fish and cake on the shore of the sea for the disciples. He served. He reached out. He supported. He counseled. He affirmed. He wept with the bereaved. He rejoiced with them that rejoiced. *Jesus did it all.* And if we are to be servants and leaders we must learn to be as the Apostle said, "all things to all men that by some means I may win them." He stayed in touch.

You cannot isolate yourself in this work. Jesus was involved. No man is an island in the kingdom of God and you see, if you get involved in the work of God, and you already are, you cannot isolate yourself. If you do not learn to communicate effectively, efficiently and properly, you will constantly vacillate from one conflict to another. You will be out of one pan of hot water into another. You'll be constantly jumping out of the frying pan into the fire. So many of the problems that we as individuals have from day to day stem from one main area and it is lack of proper understandable communication. We communicate but many times the things that we communicate by our body language or by our silence, in many instances does not truly reflect the opinion of the heart. So that is why you must always be careful that what you are saying with your lips match what your heart is saying, and what your mind is saying. You communicate by a shrug of the shoulder. You communicate by a smile or the lack of it. Communication is a fact of life and you are communicating it whether you know it or not.

We must all come to a new understanding of communication so that it can be used as a vital tool in the doing of the work of God in an expert manner. Jesus *walked* with people. He did not take the elevator. He did not just stand and watch the numbers. His questions went deeper than, what time is it? What's the date? What floor are we on? Amen.

FOOTNOTES

[1]Charles Swindoll, *Make Up Your Mind About the Issues of Life,* Multnomah Press, 1981, p. 74.

[2]Ibid., p. 74.